MARCO ⊕ POLO

LONDON

with Local Tips
The author's special recommendations are highlighted in yellow throughout this guide

There are five symbols to help you find your way around this guide:

★

Marco Polo's top recommendations – the best in each category

sites with a scenic view

where the local people meet

where young people get together

(100/A1)
pages and coordinates for the street atlas
*(**O**) outside area covered by the street atlas*

MARCO ⊕ POLO

Travel guides and language guides in this series:

Algarve • Amsterdam • Australia • Berlin • Brittany • California
Channel Islands • Costa Brava/Barcelona • Costa del Sol/Granada
Côte d'Azur • Crete • Cuba • Cyprus • Eastern USA • Florence • Florida
Gran Canaria • Greek Islands/Aegean • Ibiza • Ireland • Istanbul • Lanzarote
London • Mallorca • Malta • New York • New Zealand • Normandy • Paris
Prague • Rhodes • Rome • Scotland • South Africa • Southwestern USA
Tenerife • Turkish Coast • Tuscany • Venice • Western Canada

French • German • Italian • Spanish

Marco Polo would be very interested to hear your
comments and suggestions. Please write to:

North America:
Marco Polo North America
70 Bloor Street East
Oshawa, Ontario, Canada
(B) 905-436-2525

United Kingdom:
World Leisure Marketing Ltd
Marco Polo Guides
Newmarket Drive
Derby DE24 8 NW

Cover photograph: Image Bank: Pete Turner
Photos: British Tourist Authority (59); Kallabis (54, 72); Lade: Joke (38),
Panos (33), Pictures (68), Thompson (59), Wrba (63); Ley (99); Mauritius: Bartel (27), Cash (64),
Hubatka (98), Kabes (20), Sporting Picture (75), Vidler (14, 16, 21, 44, 46, 56, 61, 76, 82);
O'Dwyer (50, 81); Schapowalow: Atlantide (11), Heaton (5, 8); Transglobe: Giaccone (94)

1ˢᵗ edition 1999
© Mairs Geographischer Verlag, Ostfildern, Germany
Author: Annegret Schopp-O'Dwyer
Translation: Yvonne Heigl
English edition 1999: Gaia Text
Editorial director: Ferdinand Ranft
Chief editor: Marion Zorn
Cartography Street Atlas: © Mairs Geographischer Verlag; London Regional Transport
Design and layout: Thienhaus/Wippermann
Printed in Germany

CONTENTS

Discover London!

London is a city full of fascinating contrasts: home of the
Windsors — centre of avant-garde fashion
and music — a melting pot of different cultures

London impresses all its visitors although it is quite unpretentious in its own way. There is certainly a growing number of skyscrapers, but these are looked upon more with humour than with pride. This vast city does not really strive to be a metropolis — and perhaps it is precisely this which makes it one of the world's greatest cities. As well as the unique traditions of the monarchy, which are to be seen in magnificent ceremonies held in numerous historic buildings, there are countless modern attractions. This is where the latest in fashion and music, promoted by the diverse influences of a multicultural population, can be found. In the centre of the city there are spacious parks that serve as refuges from the hectic of everyday life. What

Tower Bridge:
London's world-famous
neo-Gothic landmark
from the Victorian Age

London has to offer in the way of culture is quite incomparable: more than 100 museums, 50 theatres, world-famous orchestras and opera houses — not to mention sporting events such as the tennis championships at Wimbledon, horse racing at Ascot, polo at Windsor and cricket at Lord's.

London is a conglomeration of many villages. Remains of this village structure can be seen, for example, in the numerous small green areas, which are former village commons. Most of London's development has been rather uncontrolled and even today town planning tends to be done on an ad hoc basis — an expression of British individualism. The city, which is the largest in area in Europe, is pieced together like a jigsaw puzzle, whereby every piece, every former village and present-day district or borough, has retained its own distinct personality: nonchalant, self-assured and idiosyncratic. These villages had already achieved a status of their own when the capital was still quite small: Hampstead was a famous spa before it became a district of London. In contrast to other large cities, a frenzied atmosphere is only apparent in the rush hour itself, despite 20 million visitors each year. London's Underground celebrated its centenary in 1990, making it the oldest underground railway in the world. One million commuters travel into the centre of London every day. Living in London is so expensive and the price of houses so prohibitive that commuters come from as far away as the south coast to go about their buisness in this vast city.

Present-day London extends approximately 15 kilometres (9 miles) on both sides of the river Thames. It is one of the ten largest cities in the world, with an estimated population of seven million. About 1.2 million inhabitants of London are immigrants of all nationalities, including 450,000 Asians, 350,000 Afro-Caribbeans, 230,000 Irish and other smaller ethnic groups. Add to these more than a million foreign students and countless tourists and the result is a mixture of cultures that turns a trip to this city into a world tour. These immigrants constantly provide impetus for change in a country steeped in tradition. They have enriched British culture and revolutionized its cuisine. The traditional cooking styles of immigrants from all over the world, such as Indian, Chinese, Thai and Italian, are now well-established on the London menu and lend British cuisine a new exotic taste. Afro-Caribbean rhythms are a feature of today's pop music. The influence of these 'new' British citizens can also be seen in modern dance and fashion. The Notting Hill Carnival is Europe's largest Caribbean carnival procession.

Over the centuries, London has been a place of refuge to so many people of different nationalities that numerous customs and traditions have become established here, providing invaluable enrichment for any close observer of this city. Such diversity can, of course, also lead to social tensions, such as those that led to the Brixton riots in 1981, but the proverbial British tolerance is perhaps best capable of overcoming such problems.

After 18 years of Conservative rule, a Labour government was elected with a convincing majority on 1 May 1997 and Tony Blair became Prime Minister. Much is expected of the new Labour government: on the one hand, higher taxes; on the other hand, greater social solidarity and a pro-European stance.

Alongside all these social transformations, the monarchy has survived relatively unchanged. Queen Elizabeth II is the 42nd sovereign, making Great Britain the oldest monarchy in Europe. The vast majority of the British population would not wish to see the demise of the British monarchy, although criticism is now more openly voiced. Other things remain as they always were: the British still drive on the left-hand side of the road, the famous red double-decker buses doggedly make their way through the London traffic and pub opening hours continue to vary considerably and can seem very inconvenient. An attempt to replace all the red telephone boxes with dull grey glass booths failed because of pressure from the British public, so the familiar red boxes still dot London's street corners. All these facts only add to the charm of London.

The 32 boroughs that make up Greater London cover an area of 1,867 square kilometres (720 square miles). Inner London has an area of 303 square kilometres (117 square miles). The City of London, the former Roman settlement Londinium, is the smallest borough in the town with an area of only 2.6 square kilometres (1 square mile). Only 4,600 people live in the City, whereas more than 400,000 people work here.

It is the world's leading financial centre. The Stock Exchange in London sees eight times as much trading as Wall Street and more than all the other European stock exchanges together. The Bank of England issues and destroys five million bank notes every day and watches over the country's gold reserves. Lloyd's of London is the largest insurance company in the world. The 'square mile' of banks and big business is a self-contained world enjoying the privilege of its own regulations and administration. Since 1191, its head has been the Lord Mayor of the City of London. He is elected every year by the City Livery Companies, the traditional City guilds such as goldsmiths, fishmongers,

vintners, cordwainers and tallowchandlers. These guilds are extremely conservative — women are still not allowed to become members — and they have always exercised considerable influence: they make donations to schools and in some cases even finance university professorships.

The election and installation of the Lord Mayor is celebrated every year with great pomp: the Lord Mayor's Show, the procession of the newly elected Lord Mayor in a ceremonial coach accompanied by pikemen and various floats, takes place on the second Saturday in November. The livery companies also take part in the parade, decked out in their magnificent robes.

London is also Britain's media centre. The main television and radio companies, including the BBC (British Broadcasting Corporation), are all based here. All the national daily and Sunday newspapers are published in London, although Fleet Street is gradually losing its reputation as London's 'street of ink', the journalists' street. Many newspaper companies have moved out to the Docklands in the course of the technical modernization of the press.

The Times has been based in Wapping since 1986, the *Daily Mail* has moved out to the Surrey Docks and the *Daily Telegraph* and the *Guardian* are now on the Isle of Dogs. This all means the end of a very old tradition: the first printing presses were introduced to Fleet Street at the end of the 15th century by an apprentice of William Caxton, Wynkyn de Worde, who

Big Ben chimes hourly, but the red double-decker buses are seldom on time

produced 600 books here in 35 years. The first national daily newspaper was printed here in 1702. This is where the *Times* celebrated its 200th anniversary in 1985.

Indeed, the British parliament is known as the 'Mother of Parliaments'. The signing of the Magna Carta in 1215, which protected the rights of the barons and churchmen against encroachment by the royal prerogative, is viewed by some as having laid the foundation for a democratic constitution. The original Magna Carta can be viewed in the British Museum.

It is not surprising that some of the richest people in the world own property in London. For instance, the Duke of Westminster possesses 150 hectares (370 acres) in Mayfair. These estates date back to the year 1677 and form the basis of a fortune of £4,200 million. Incidentally, the Queen is the richest woman in the world with a fortune of £3,340 million.

London is almost 2,000 years old – and its history reflects the development of Great Britain. It was first settled in Roman times when the trading centre of Londinium was founded on the north bank of the River Thames in A.D. 42. Later, the country was invaded and occupied by Anglo-Saxons and Vikings. There are very few remains from this time. The most interesting are in the church building of All Hallows-by-the-Tower and in the crypt of St Stephen's Chapel in the old Palace of Westminster. In the 11th century the Normans conquered England. Every child in Britain knows the significance of 1066. This was the year in which William the Conqueror defeated Harold at the Battle of Hastings. William was crowned King of England in Westminster Abbey that same year. He commissioned the building of the White Tower, the core of the Tower of London, as a fortress and as a sign of his military strength. His son, William Rufus, had Westminster Hall added to the Palace of Westminster. London became the official capital of England.

The 12th century was characterized by power struggles between the landed nobility and the monarchy. The Hundred Years' War with France began in 1337. These were turbulent times, in which the Black Death killed a quarter of the population of England in 1348. Nevertheless, London continued to expand. Rich landowners built houses along the bank, the 'Strand', of the Thames near the king's palace at Westminster. Lawyers took up residence in hostels or inns, such as Gray's Inn and Lincoln's Inn, and rich merchants built great mansions in the old part of the city. Henry VIII, also famous for his six wives, broke with the church in Rome in 1534, which meant that the English sovereign was now the supreme head of the Church of England.

The subsequent dissolution of the monasteries provided Henry VIII and the nobility with more land for development and it was at this time that Hampton Court Palace and St James's Palace were built. The Elizabethan Age (1558–1603) that followed is regarded as the heyday of English history and culture, which culminated in the plays of William Shakespeare. This was a time of maritime expansion and exploration by such men as Sir Francis Drake, the English naval hero and adventurer in the service of the queen, and Sir Walter Raleigh, who founded the first English colony in North America. But it was also in Elizabeth's reign that Mary Stuart, the Catholic queen of Scotland who had raised claims to the English throne, was executed. In 1605, Guy Fawkes and other Catholics formed the Gunpowder Plot to blow up James I and parliament.

The conspirators were discovered in time. Religious conflicts in the reigns of the early Stuart kings, which were also related to power struggles between parliament and the monarchy, culminated in civil war. Charles I was beheaded in 1649 and Cromwell established his repressive puritan Commonwealth. England blossomed again after the restoration of the Stuart dynasty in 1660. London had in the meantime almost half a million inhabitants.

In 1665, a renewed outbreak of the plague claimed more than 100,000 victims in London. One year later, the Great Fire of London raged for four days and destroyed most of the city, which had consisted of closely-built timber houses. Numerous plans were submitted for the imaginative construction of a new city, but the speed required to provide the population with new homes meant that building went ahead on the old street plan. Christopher Wren, London's best represented if not most important architect, designed more than 20 churches and other important buildings that were completed within the next seven years. Today these Jacobean or English Renaissance-style buildings can be admired throughout the city.

Wren's greatest masterpiece is St Paul's Cathedral. The 17th century saw development on the estates of several London magnates, such as in the St James and Piccadilly areas; for instance the Earl of Bedford had an Italian-style piazza laid out on his property at Covent Garden. The Georgian period was a time of expansion especially in the West End in the areas of Mayfair and Marylebone, where elegant town houses were erected. Most of London's squares were laid out at this time. Hyde Park, St James's Park and Regent's Park, once royal hunting grounds, were gradually opened to the public. New bridges were built to span the Thames in the late 18th and early 19th centuries. London, the commercial and political heart of an expanding empire, was the leading city of the Western world. The Victorian or neo-Gothic architectural style of this age can best be seen in the Housses of Parliament. The population of London soared in Victorian times and the poor lived in cramped and squalid slums. However, the advent of the railways in the 19th century helped to alleviate this situation as people began to move out of the centre to the suburbs and London expanded dramatically in all directions.

London suffered little material damage in World War I, but German air-raids during World War II devastated whole areas and many historic buildings. The docks, the East End and the City were worst-hit; more than 30,000 people were killed. In the mid-'70s, Richard Rogers, the architect of the Pompidou Centre in Paris, designed the new Lloyd's Building. Other modern buildings followed and London's appearance began to change dramatically with the growth of other gigantic office blocks within the City. London Docklands is Europe's greatest inner-city development project, covering more than 2,000 hectares (5,000 acres) of land and water-filled docks, from Tower Bridge to the Thames Barrier. Britain's tallest building, Canary Wharf Tower (244 m/800 ft), was completed here in 1991. The traditional and modern have always existed side by side in this city. It takes some time to discover all the different facets of London. Much is hidden, waiting to be discovered. It is important to watch and listen carefully to gain a true impression of this metropolis.

The majority of visitors to London will, of course, want to see the most famous tourist attractions first. So here is a short introduction to give you a first impression of the most important sights, for no tourist should leave London without having seen Westminster Abbey and Big Ben, not to mention St Paul's and the Tower. Buckingham Palace is best approached via Pall Mall, a wonderful tree-lined avenue with houses designed by John Nash that sparkle in white and form the backdrop for many

The market halls of Covent Garden are a popular meeting place

of the royal parades. Take a look at Carlton House Terrace on the way, where such famous people as Lord Curzon, Earl Gray and Prime Minister Gladstone once lived. If the weather is fine, it is worth spending some time in St James's Park, an oasis of peace where you can relax in a deck chair or lie out on the grass. Plan to arrive at Buckingham Palace at about eleven o'clock in the morning in order to secure a place at the front of the railings for the Changing of the Guard. Since 1993, part of the palace has been open to the public. Once a year, the Queen invites a maximum of 9,000 chosen guests to a garden party, when ordinary people can enjoy a stroll among the flamingos and flower borders. (It is also possible to view the gardens from the roof-top restaurant of the Hilton Hotel in Park Lane.) If you cross St James's Park in the direction of Horse Guards Road, you can visit the Cabinet War Rooms, Winston Churchill's underground command centre during World War II, on the corner of King Charles Street, which leads to Whitehall and to No. 10 Downing Street, the official residence of the British Prime Minister. The Houses of Parliament, Westminster Abbey and Big Ben are all best viewed first from Westminster Bridge.

The Tower, the oldest Norman fortress in England, is another absolute must for tourists. Notorious for the many prisoners who were executed there, it should be approached with due respect and with a lot of time in hand — the Tower is the most popular of all the tourist attractions. After a tour of the fortress, it is worthwhile enjoying a view of the Thames and a large part of London from Tower Bridge. Those with enough energy left can walk on past the Tower Hotel to St Katharine Dock. These old docks with their traditional warehouses and old sailing ships are now an attractive business and leisure centre and provide a foretaste of London's latest development project: the Docklands.

The best way to explore London is on foot. You might want to follow the London Silver Jubilee Walkway, which is 7.5 kilometres (12 miles) long and encompasses all the important sights in central London. This walk was laid out in 1977 to commemorate Queen Elizabeth II's 25th jubilee. It is marked throughout by the Silver Jubilee symbol so that it is possible to begin anywhere en route. Take along a map with explanations of the route, which can be obtained from the London Tourist Board. The walk leads past the London Dungeon, the museum of horrors. After a visit here allow yourself some time to recover in the George Inn, the only surviving galleried inn in London. Located as it was between Shakespeare's Globe Theatre (the reconstruction of which was opened in 1996), beer houses and brothels, the George was already quite well known for its good food in Shakespeare's time.

It is easy to imagine what London must have been like in earlier times. The London fog, which features in the stories of Charles Dickens and conjures up the wretched conditions of the early 19th century, is famous all over the world. Oliver Twist, David Copperfield, Scrooge are all characters who can never be forgotten. Sir Arthur Conan Doyle's fictitious Sherlock Holmes almost seems like a real detective to many people who zealously follow his trail: 'his' house at 221 b Baker Street; the wild chases in the Café Royal in Piccadilly or at the Charing Cross Hotel, where he was wounded; and the Sherlock Holmes Pub in Northumber-landAvenue. There is even a Sherlock Holmes Society that is dedicated to his memory.

Director Alfred Hitchcock's first sound film, *Blackmail* (1929), finishes with the blackmailer's spectacular fall through the dome of the Reading Room at the British Museum. This thriller shows a sombre Piccadilly Circus and Trafalgar Square. Early Charlie Chaplin films are also set in the poorer areas of London – in the bleak East End of the '20s.

Covent Garden appears in Hitchcock's *Frenzy* as it was before its yuppification: a fruit and vegetable market without any romantic traces, even if Eliza Doolittle did find Professor Higgins there. The rise in social status of this flower girl in *My Fair Lady,* which occurs at Ascot, provides a picture of the bright side of London. In John Wayne's *Brannigan,* Leadenhall Market is almost demolished and James Bond races through Whitehall in *A View to a Kill.*

Time and again writers have striven to express the phenomenon of London in words. Their conflicting impressions show the peculiar fascination of this city: 'By seeing London I have seen as much of life as the world has to show' (Samuel Johnson). 'Hell is a city much like London – a populous and smoky city with little justice and less pity' (Percy Bysshe Shelley). 'London, the flower of cities all!' (William Dunbar). 'Nobody is healthy in London. Nobody can be' (Jane Austen). 'Send a philosopher to London and not a poet ... this utter seriousness about all things, this terrible monotony ... this moroseness which strangles all joy, this excessive London suffocates the imagination and rends one's heart ...' (Heinrich Heine).

London has been the home of many poets. Writers from all over the world have lived and worked here – so many, in fact, that the *Guide to Literary London* has almost 400 pages!

Perhaps everyone should experience this city for the first time as William Wordsworth did – in the early morning light:
'Earth has not anything to show more fair:
Dull would he be of soul who could pass by
A sight so touching in its majesty:
This City now doth, like a garment, wear the beauty of the morning; silent, bare,
Ships, towers, domes, theatres, and temples lie
Open unto the fields, and to the sky;
All bright and glittering in the smokeless air.'

William Wordsworth (1770–1850) on 3 September 1802

What to see ?

London has endless attractions: enchanting parks and palaces, monumental buildings and bridges, famous streets and squares

It is impossible to see everything in London. That would take years. Everyone must choose what interests him most. You can often combine getting somewhere with sightseeing, for instance a trip on the No. 159 bus through London in order to gain a first impression of the city or a boat trip past historic Westminster to the Docklands, the financial centre of the future. The *tube*, the underground railway with 271 stations, is the easiest and quickest way of getting around London. With the aid of a *journey planner*, a pocket map of the Underground that is available from any Underground station, or the map in this guide, you should be able to find your way around the Underground quite easily. This is a faster means of transport than the red buses, which seldom run on time. Of course, there are London's world-famous taxis, which can

be hailed in the street when the yellow sign is illuminated. For a group of three or four people travelling together this is not much more expensive than any other means of transport. *London Walks (Tel: 0171-624 39 79)* or *Historical Walks (Tel: 0181-668 40 19)* offer a wide variety of conducted walking tours.

ARCHITECTURAL HIGHLIGHTS & MONUMENTS

Big Ben (112/A3)

⧖ London's famous landmark. The vast Big Ben bell weighs 13 tons and hangs in a 97 metre (318 foot) high clock tower — there are 334 steps! It chimes punctually on the hour in 'Westminster time'. A light in the clock tower at night means that parliament is still 'sitting'. *Parliament Square; Underground: Westminster*

Buckingham Palace (111/D–E2–3)

Queen Victoria was the first sovereign to live here and the palace has been the London home of the Royal Family ever since. The Royal Standard flies above the

At one time there was a busy market in front of St Paul's Cathedral

Buckingham Palace: the Royal Standard flies when the Queen is in residence

palace when the Queen is in residence, while the Union Jack flies at all times. The famous ceremony of the *Changing of the Guard* takes place at 11.30 am — it is best to get there early to have a good view. If you miss seeing the 'busbies' here, they can also be seen at Windsor Castle. Originally built in the 18th century as a town house for the Duke of Buckingham, Buckingham Palace has since been remodelled by three different architects, including John Nash. The east façade (the side seen by the public) was redesigned in Neoclassical style in 1913 — but looks rather more pompous than elegant. Part of the palace has been open to the public since 1993 *(long queues, admission £8, tickets can be booked in advance at the Visitors Office up until 11 March each year)*. The Queen's Gallery at the south end of the palace exhibits selections from the Queen's collection of paintings. *Queen's Gallery; Tues-Sat 11 am–5 pm, Sun 2 pm–5 pm; Buckingham Palace Road; Underground: Charing Cross/Victoria*

Cable Street Mural (107/E6)

Commemorates the street fighting in which 100,000 East Enders along with their Jewish neighbours stopped the march of Sir Oswald Mosley's Fascist party on 5 October 1936. The street barrier set up by the anti-Fascists — 'They shall not pass!' was their motto — was on the corner of Royal Mint Street and Dock Street. Even the police who had been escorting the Mosley demonstrators were stopped. This area is interesting today for the contrasting co-existence of the old East End and Tobacco Dock, part of the dramatic conversion of the former Docklands. *236 Cable Street; Docklands Light Railway: Shadwell; bus 100 from Tower Hill, bus 15 from Oxford Circus to Shadwell station*

Cleopatra's Needle (112/B1)

This obelisk of granite from Heliopolis in Egypt stands just over 18 metres (60 feet) high on the Victoria Embankment. It was carved in 1475 B.C., making it the oldest monument in London. A present from the Turkish Viceroy of Egypt, the 186-ton monolith was transported to London by boat in 1878. (It has no connection with Cleopatra apart from its country of origin.) *Underground: Embankment*

Guildhall (105/F5)

The town hall of the City of London dates from 1411, although only parts of the façade and the Great Hall have survived from the original building. Municipal meetings (open to the public) are held here every third Thursday at 1 pm. It is in the Guildhall that members of the City Livery Companies elect the Sheriffs and the Lord Mayor of the City of London. The liverymen dress in their magnificent robes for all official occasions and state banquets. Incidentally, the old-fashioned and very elegant toilets in the Guildhall are well worth a visit! The Museum of the 'Worshipful Company of Clockworkers' is

---

MARCO POLO SELECTION:
SIGHTSEEING

housed in the newer section of the Guildhall and contains clocks and watches from several centuries. Another beautiful building is the Armourers' Hall in Moorgate, on the corner of Coleman Street. *Mon–Fri 10 am–5 pm; Gresham Street; Underground: Bank*

Houses of Parliament (112/A2–3)

Its official name is 'The Palace of Westminster'. This was the site of the principal royal residence from the time of Edward the Confessor to that of Henry VIII (1509–47). The magnificent Westminster Hall has survived from the old palace; its hammer-beam roof weighs about 660 tons. This was the site of the chief law court in England. Thomas More and Charles I were condemned to death in this hall; Oliver Cromwell was proclaimed lord protector here. The old palace was destroyed by fire in 1834 and rebuilt in neo-Gothic style. It has been the seat of the English parliament — the 'cradle of democracy' — since 1547. The present building covers an area of 3.2 hectares (8 acres) and its two halves show how the parliamentary system in England has developed. The Lords (1,300) sit in the House of Lords, the Upper House, and the Commoners (635) in the House of Commons, the Lower House. The Commoners met for some years in St Stephen's Chapel, which explains the form of the Lower House. Present-day representatives of the people complain about the lack of space — more than 2,000 people work in the 'House'. There are always long queues of visitors outside (St Stephen's entrance). To avoid them, contact your embassy for a 'card of introduction' (three months in advance). Open only when parliament is in session. *House of Commons Mon–Thurs from 4 pm, Fri from 10 am; House of Lords Mon–Wed from 2.30 pm, Thurs from 3 pm; Parliament Square; Underground: Westminster*

Lloyd's of London (106/B5)

Designed by Richard Rogers, it was built in 1986 at a cost of £200 million. The new headquarters of Lloyd's insurance company shocked many Londoners; others think it is wonderful. Twelve floors of galleries are arranged round a central building made of glass that has been specially treated so that it glitters like crystal no matter what the weather is like. All the technical installations that are normally hidden, such as the heating pipes, have been incorporated in six smaller towers surrounding the main building. Visitors travel up the outside of the building in glass lifts to reach an atrium with an area of 2,800 square metres (30,000 square feet) and a height of 73 metres (240 feet). Lloyd's has insured such valuable items as Marlene Dietrich's and Marilyn Monroe's legs. It is the largest insurance market in the world. *It has not been open to the public since the IRA bomb attack; Lime Street; Underground: Aldgate/Monument*

Old Bailey (105/E5)

✦ The notorious Newgate Prison stood on this site. Dickens, Chesterton, Edgar Wallace, Agatha Christie and George Orwell all included it in their novels. It was replaced by the 'Central Criminal Court' in 1902, where most of the major trials are heard. The public may view the proceedings in Courts I to III by queuing for a seat in the Public Gallery. Access to the courts is from Newgate Street. *Mon–Fri 10 am–1 pm and 2 pm–4 pm; Old Bailey Street; Underground: St Paul's/ Blackfriars*

Royal Albert Hall and Albert Memorial   (109/E3)
Queen Victoria laid the foundation stone of the building named after her beloved Prince Albert in 1867 and it was subsequently opened in 1871. This immense oval amphitheatre has a diameter of 91 metres (300 feet) and seating capacity for 7,000 spectators. Concerts, balls and sporting events are all held here. The 'Proms', the Promenade Concerts that have taken place here every year since 1895, are very famous and extremely popular (long queues). ★ *The Last Night of the Proms* shows the British in a completely different light for once: waving flags and singing along to 'Rule Britannia' with great enthusiasm. The Albert Memorial opposite depicts the prince reading a catalogue of the Great Exhibition of 1851. 'Dear Albert', mourned by Queen Victoria for 40 years, is at his best in spring, surrounded by the crocuses and daffodils in Kensington Gardens. *Kensington Gore; Underground: South Kensington*

Smithfield Market   (104/D4)
★ The London meat market is located in a beautiful Victorian cast-iron market hall. Medieval tournaments took place on the 'Smoothfield' in the 14th century, when knights from France, Flanders and the Rhine area came to test their strength. It was also used as an execution ground from the 12th century on. The Bartholomew Fair, the market and medieval fair immortalized by Ben Jonson, was held here every August for 700 years. Today the market has an annual turnover of some 350,000 tons of produce, which makes it one of the largest meat, poultry and provision markets in the world. Best times to visit are *Mon–Wed 8 am–11 am; West Smithfield; Underground: Farringdon/St Paul's*

Temple – Inns of Court   (104/B5)
★ The English seat of the Knights Templar, the powerful military and religious order, in the 12th and 13th centuries. Today this extensive enclosed area is the centre of English jurisprudence. There are four law schools, 'Inns of Court', here: Middle Temple and Inner Temple as well as the adjacent Lincoln's Inn and Gray's Inn. Every Inn has its own magnificent buildings set around inner courtyards and large gardens. Barristers with flowing robes and powdered wigs disappear down endless crooked lanes on their way to their chambers – a scene reminiscent of Dickens. The King's Bench Walk in the Inner Temple is particularly romantic. House No. 4 was the town house of Vita Sackville-West, the scandal-seeker of the Bloomsbury Group. Dickens worked for a while in the Old Buildings of Lincoln's Inn as an unhappy clerk. This is where Thomas More, Oliver Cromwell, William Pitt, Disraeli, Gladstone and Margaret Thatcher all studied.

The Old Hall contains what must be the most splendid carved oak ceiling in London (ask the porter). In Lincoln's Inn Fields is the Sir John Soane's Museum (1753–1837), the private house of a genius and eccentric, distinguished architect (of the Dulwich College Picture Gallery, the Bank of England, the British Museum) and an indefatigable collector. Be sure to see the white alabaster sarcophagus of Seti I from Thebes (approx. 1300 B.C.) and paintings by Turner, Canaletto and Hogarth. A colourful mixture of styles and treasures from all over the world. The Breakfast Room is particularly interesting. *Tues–Sat 10 am–5 pm; 13 Lincoln's Inn Fields; Underground: Temple/Aldwych/Chancery Lane/Holborn*

Thames Barrier (O)

Built between 1975 and 1982 at a cost of £500 million, this gigantic silver barrier is designed to protect London from flooding. The futuristic steel capsules – reminiscent of the Opera House in Sydney – can raise ten 20 metre (65 foot) high gates and so completely 'shut off' London within 30 minutes. The world's largest movable flood barrier stretches 520 metres (1,700 feet) across the Thames. With the amount of concrete that was used here it would have been possible to build 15 kilometres (9 miles) of a six-lane motorway! It is worthwhile taking a short boat trip from the Visitors Centre. *British Rail: from Charing Cross Station to Charlton; from Greenwich, Westminster or Tower Pier by boat in approx. 90 minutes; Visitors Centre; Mon–Fri 10.30 am–5 pm; Sat and Sun 10.30 am–5.30 pm*

Tower of London (106/B6)

The Tower is surely the most impressive building in London. It is 30 metres (100 feet) high and its walls are up to 3.6 metres (12 feet) thick. The Tower was used as a royal residence from William the Conqueror to

The Thames Barrier gates can be raised 20 metres (65 ft) high to protect London from flooding

The Tower of London still commands respect today

James I (1603–25). This was the site of the first observatory, the Crown Jewels, the Royal Mint, the Royal Arsenal and even the Royal Menagerie in later days. The enormous grey fortress is best known, however, for its many famous prisoners: Ann Boleyn, Henry VIII's second wife, was confined here before she was beheaded; Sir Walter Raleigh, the founder of Virginia, was imprisoned here for 13 years before his execution! '-Bloody Mary', Henry VIII's daughter — the drink of the same name is called after her — had countless opponents of her rule executed on Tower Hill. The last famous prisoner in the Tower was Rudolf Hess, Hitler's deputy, who was detained in the Queen's House. The oldest part of the fortress is the Norman White Tower, which now houses the 'Royal Armoury'. The Crown Jewels are in the ★ Jew-

el House, which is visited every day by expectant onlookers. Outstanding exhibits here are the 530-carat 'Star of Africa' in the Sovereign's Sceptre, the largest cut diamond in the world, Queen Victoria's crown, set with 3,000 jewels, and the Queen Mother's crown, which includes the famous Indian Diamond, the Koh-i-noor. The ravens are all that remains of the menagerie that was moved to Regent's Park in 1835. As legend has it, if the ravens ever leave the Tower, then the Tower will fall! Their wings are therefore clipped and they are well cared for. The Tower is 'guarded' by the *Beefeaters*, the Yeoman Warders in traditional red Tudor uniforms. Beside the Tower is Tower Green, the former execution ground. A black granite slab marks the spot where the block once stood. Only royalty was beheaded here. Members of the aristocracy were executed on Tower Hill and the common people were hanged on the Tyburn gallows at Marble Arch — such fine distinctions were preserved even in death. Long queues (for everyone)! *Mar–Oct Mon–Sat 9.30 am–5 pm, Sun 10 am–5pm; Nov–Feb Mon– Sat 9.30 am–4 pm; Underground: Tower Hill*

Trocadero   (111/E1)
☆ Hidden behind a classical façade is the most modern entertainment centre in London. Everything imaginable in the *virtual-reality* spectrum is here: *Segaworld* — an interactive theme park with six floors of rides and experiences, Lazer Bowl in Fundland, Max Drop, a Rock Circus, the Emaginator and the

UK's first Imax 3D cinema. *Trocadero Center, Piccadilly; Underground: Piccadilly*

BRIDGES

The London Bridge and Tower Bridge are the most famous of London's 17 bridges. The modern Chelsea Bridge and Hammersmith Bridge are also very beautiful, full of frills and decorations, and the Albert Bridge is particularly pretty when it is lit up at night.

London Bridge (113/F1)

London's oldest bridge — there was a wooden bridge slightly to the east of here in Roman times. The famous London Bridge of stone was finished in 1209 and remained the only bridge over the Thames in London until 1739. In this century, the London Bridge dating from 1831 was bought by an American oil company and rebuilt in Lake Havasu City, Arizona. Apparently it had been confused with the Tower Bridge! The present structure was completed in 1972. *Underground: Monument*

Tower Bridge (114/B1)

↘ The most famous bridge in Europe in the fairy-tale style of Victorian Gothic (1894). It is a masterpiece of engineering: the centre piece, two drawbridges each weighing 1,100 tons, can be opened in 90 seconds. The two towers provide magnificent panoramic views of London. The newly opened museum houses an exhibition centering on the bridge's history. *Underground: Tower Hill*

CEMETERIES

Brompton Cemetery (O)

This is the largest cemetery in London with more than 204,000 graves. It is the burial place of the Chelsea Pensioners. Emmeline Pankhurst, the champion of women's rights, and the singer Richard Tauber are also buried here. The loveliest grave is that of Frederick Leyland, whose magnificent tombstone was designed by Pre-Raphaelite artist Edward Burne-Jones. *Underground: Earl's Court*

Golders Green Cemetery/Crematorium (O)

Here are the graves of the famous cellist Jacqueline Dupré and of Jo Collins, the father of actress Joan Collins. Peter Sellers, the comedian, and pop stars Marc Bolan and Keith Moon are also buried here as is Freud and his family. *Hoop Lane; Underground: Golders Green, follow the sign for the crematorium*

Highgate Cemetery (O)

★ London's prettiest cemetery. It is particularly famous for the grave of Karl Marx. Anna Mahler, the actor Ralph Richardson as well as novelist George Eliot are also buried here. On the western side are the graves of the Dickens family and that of Michael Faraday, the famous chemist. In all, 166,000 people are buried here. The eastern side of the cemetery can be visited daily from 10 am to 4 pm (a small fee is charged); admission to the western side is only possible with the guided tours that are conducted every hour. Romantic Waterlow Park is directly adjacent to the cemetery. *Tel: 0181-340 18 34, or Friends of Highgate Cemetery, Tel: 0181-348 08 08; Swaine's Lane, Highgate; Underground: Archway, another 15 minutes on foot*

CHURCHES

The architectural style of the majority of churches in London can be explained by one very specific event: on 2 September 1666, a fire broke out in Pudding Lane, in the present-day City. Fanned by the wind, it rapidly developed into a gigantic inferno that engulfed five-sixths of the medieval town. Today there are only five medieval churches in London. Charles II commissioned the royal architect Christopher Wren to draw up plans for the reconstruction of the City. Wren designed numerous public buildings, most of which were churches. His work typifies the spirit of the Reformation: stained glass windows or other elements that would separate the priest from the congregation or divert their attention were not allowed. Wren's churches are famous for their tall church spires, designed to stretch high into the heavens.

A tradition from which tourists benefit is that of *lunchtime* concerts, which are held in many of the churches, particularly in the City, from 12.30 pm to 1.30 pm. Admission to these is free. A list of these concerts is available from the Guildhall every month *(Events in the City; Tel: 0171-606 30 30)*. The best known lunchtime concerts are held in the churches St Mary-le-Bow, Cheapside, and the Church of the Holy Sepulchre without Newgate, Holborn Viaduct. Please remember that English churches have to pay for their own upkeep and that donations are therefore always welcome.

All Hallows-by-the-Tower (106/B6)
This is London's oldest church and it contains relics dating from the year A.D. 675. Its tower survived the bombs of World War II; it was from here that the diarist Samuel Pepys saw 'the saddest sight of desolation' caused by the Great Fire in 1666. In the undercroft museum are various exhibits from London's 2,000-year-old history. These include a model of Roman London, Roman coins, fragments of Roman paving, part of the original wall of the church and the remains of two Saxon crosses. *Byward Street; Underground: Tower Hill*

All Saints (103/E5)
A late Victorian gem commissioned by the Oxford movement, which under Catholic influences produced this rather bombastic style. *Margaret Street; Underground: Oxford Circus*

The Mandir (O)
The largest Hindu temple outside of India was built here in three years by 1,000 construction workers using marble from Carrara and other costly materials — a fata morgana in the suburb of Neasden. *Phone in advance to arrange a visit; Tel: 0181-965 26 51; 54–62 Meadow Garth, Brentfield Road; Underground: Neasden*

St Bride's Church (105/D6)
Long known as the Parish Church of the Press. Following an air raid in 1940 the remains of a Roman house were uncovered in the ruins. These can now be seen in the crypt. It was discovered that a church had been founded on this site in the 6th century by St Bridget, an Irish saint from Kildare. This means that it was the first Christian church in England. After the building was completely destroyed in the Great Fire, one of the first of Wren's churches was built here. Its spire, originally with a height of 71 metres (234 feet), the tallest steeple of all the City churches, has been called a 'madrigal in stone'. The creator of the sentimental novel, Samuel Richardson, is buried in St Bride's churchyard. *Fleet Street; Underground: Blackfriars*

St Helen's Bishopsgate (105/F5)
In this church it is possible to order *lunch* a few days in advance and eat it in the nave along with 600 others who come here on Tuesdays and Thursdays. St Helen's dates from the 12th century and has numerous graves and monuments, including the grave of Sir Thomas Gresham, who founded the Royal Exchange. *Tel: 0171-283 22 31; Bishopsgate; Underground: Aldgate/ Bank*

St Martin-in-the-Fields (112/A1)
This world-famous church on Trafalgar Square was built by James Gibbs from 1722 to 1726. Buckingham Palace is within the parish boundaries, and there are royal boxes at the east end of the church. It has an excellent classical orchestra, the Academy of St Martin-in-the-Fields. During World War II, the crypt served as an air-raid shelter. These days, part of it is a shelter for the homeless. *Trafalgar Square; Underground: Charing Cross*

St Mary-le-Strand (112/A1)
This small Baroque church, which stands on an island site in the Strand, is very much worth a visit. It was built by the architect James Gibbs in the early 18th century and is one of the best examples of Italian-influenced church architecture in London. Damaged by bombs in World War II, and by present-day pollution, it is threatened by decay despite aid from Prince Charles. *Strand; Underground: Aldwych*

St Paul's Cathedral (105/E5)
★ This magnificent building is a huge structure, 157 metres (515 feet) long and crowned by a beautiful central dome that rises to 111 metres (365 feet) above ground level. Its history can be traced back to the year 604. Old St Paul's, William II's Norman monument, was even larger than the present-day cathedral! In the Middle Ages, St Paul's Cross became the seat of lawyers — Carlyle called St Paul's Church the 'Times of the Middle Ages'. Papal bulls were proclaimed from its pulpit; Ridley and Latimer, two bishops who were later burned at the stake on the orders of Mary I, both preached here. Henry VIII allowed the church to fall into disrepair and it eventually be-

came a market place — services were still held in the midst of the crowds! In the reign of Charles I, Inigo Jones was able to restore the building to its former glory — then came Cromwell, who used the cathedral as an army barracks. His troops destroyed a large part of the building — even the ceiling fell down! Charles II commissioned Christopher Wren with the restoration of the building in 1666. It took 35 years to complete. St Paul's Cathedral became the masterpiece of the most famous architect in England. His tombstone in the crypt carries the epitaph: 'Reader, if you seek a monument, look about you'. A message whispered on one side of the 'Whispering Gallery' can be heard 30 metres (100 ft) away on the other side. The wooden choir stalls and organ frame were carved by Grinling Gibbons; Handel and Mendelssohn both played on the organ here. Lord Nelson and the Duke of Wellington are buried in the crypt, the longest in Europe. *Admission charge; St Paul's Churchyard; Underground: St Paul's*

Westminster Abbey (112/A3)

Coronation church of almost all the English sovereigns since William the Conqueror and burial place of many kings and queens as well as several of their subjects. In all, there are 1,000 or so monuments in the Abbey that commemorate great names from Britain's past. The original Norman church was rebuilt in 1245 in French Gothic style; its design was modelled on that of French cathedrals such as Reims and Amiens. A highlight, despite

the admission charge, not to be missed: the chapel of Henry VII, the culmination of the Perpendicular style (English Late Gothic), where Elizabeth I and Mary Stuart are buried. The chapel roof, with its intricate and lace-like fan vaulting, is one of the finest of its kind. *Broad Sanctuary; Underground: Westminster*

DISTRICTS

Bloomsbury (104/A3)

Gained renown in this century through its association with the 'Bloomsbury Group' centred around Virginia Woolf. She lived at 46 Gordon Square. E. M. Forster, whose novels about India have been filmed by David Lean, as well as Bertrand Russell, Aldous Huxley and W. B. Yeats all lived in Bloomsbury around 1910. It charms the visitor with its Georgian architecture, ordered rows of terraced houses and pretty squares such as Bedford Square and Bloomsbury Square. This is the site of the British Museum, the University of London, the Slade School of Fine Arts, an internationally renowned academy, as well as numerous second-hand bookshops and publishers, as well as a Baroque church designed by N. Hawksmoor: *St George, Bloomsbury Way*. One of the best bookshops in London is *Dillons, 82 Gower Street*. For lovers of Chinese porcelain: *The Percival David Foundation of Chinese Art, 53 Gordon Square*. Charles Dickens wrote several of his novels while living in Tavistock Square between 1851 and 1869. Not far from Gray's Inn Road are the Inns of Court,

Underground: Temple. Coram Fields was the site of the largest Foundling Hospital in London, established by Thomas Coram. Among the founders and Governors of the school were the artists Hogarth, Gainsborough, Reynolds and Handel, who was also conductor of the children's choir here. *Underground: Holborn*

Brixton (O)

The centre of the Afro-Caribbean immigrant population lies between Brixton Station Road and Coldharbour Lane. Since the riots of 1981 the name of this district has been associated with rebellious young black people, although only 29 per cent of the population consists of Afro-Caribbeans and Asians. In recent years Brixton has attempted to cast off its image of social unrest. Modern reggae, rap, house and other pop clubs, such as the Brixton Academy with room for 4,000 guests and *the Fridge,* attract young people from all over London. Brixton's new self-assurance shows itself in music and fashion. A walk around Brixton is informative. Just do not appear too curious in the area around Railton Road known as the *frontline.* Fascinating: *Electric Avenue,* the first street to have electric lighting in London, for Brixton was a popular shopping and residential district in 1888. At *Brixton Market* in *Atlantic Road* you can buy Caribbean fruit and vegetables; African-inspired clothing, jewellery and music are to be found in *Granville Arcade.* A sign of past times is the Ritzy Cinema in Art Nouveau style, which shows a good selection of films, especially on Thursdays. The Brixton Fashion Centre in Effra Road and the Brixton Enterprise Centre sell everything — from rubber jackets to wedding dresses. Multicultural contemporary art is displayed in the *Brixton Artist Collective, Unit 10, Brixton Station Road.* And the best pizzas in south London can be bought at the *Pizzeria Franco* in Market Row. *Buses: 2, 2A and 3 run from central London to Railton Road; Underground: Brixton*

Covent Garden (104/A5)

★ ☆ Formerly London's vegetable market — since 1980 a promenade area, especially popular with young people. The area around Neal Street, Neal's Yard, where London's first alternative shops have held out against the inner-city conversion, is especially interesting. There are all kinds of kites in *The Kite Store.* The *Belgo* restaurant serves mussels and 'monks' — try them! Don't miss *The Tea House*, which has an enormous selection of teapots. The Smith Gallery has contemporary art. The *Donmar Warehouse*, a very good fringe theatre, is located in the middle of the stylish *Thomas Neal Shopping Centre.* There are all kinds of shops inside the old market halls. The Jubilee Market, with craft, jewellery, bric-a-brac and clothes stalls, is held every day. The Royal Opera House, London's internationally famous opera house, is in St James's Street, on the corner of Floral Street (closed for refurbishment at the moment). Behind the market lies the London Transport Museum. One of the

Enjoy some fascinating views of the Docklands on a train journey to the Isle of Dogs

oldest theatres in London, The Theatre Royal, is situated in Drury Lane. Pantomimists, musicians and jugglers all perform in Covent Garden, one of the liveliest districts in London. Sitting in the *Opera Terrace Café* high above the market sipping a 'Pimm's' on a sunny evening — the perfect combination of traditional and modern life-styles. *Underground: Covent Garden*

Docklands (O)

★ London's former Docklands have been undergoing a most remarkable transformation for the past ten years — this is the biggest building site in Europe! Damage suffered during the war, a rigid labour market policy and new means of transport resulted in the Port of London being moved to Tilbury — the area between Tower Bridge and Woolwich lay empty and disused. Following the successful redevelopment of the St Katharine Dock, the consequences of a generous tax and planning policy are now becoming apparent on the Isle of Dogs. Modern buildings covered by reflecting glass alternate with architectural monstrosities of a bygone age. In Canary Wharf stands the tallest building in Great Britain: Canary Wharf Tower. Tobacco Dock has been converted into the first *shopping village* — only a few minutes away from the old East End. *The Times* in Wapping and the *Daily*

Telegraph building in Millwall Dock bear witness to the newspaper companies' move away from Fleet Street. Even an airport, the London City Airport, has been built. After the stock exchange crash in 1987 the yuppies' *(young urban professionals)* mood was subdued and the prices of flats fell. Problems with the infrastructure have not yet been solved, and social conflicts accompany the conversion of run-down housing areas into luxury residential areas beside the water. Improvements are only gradually setting in – the birth of the new district is taking longer than planned. *Docklands Light Railway: South Quay; Information Centre in Lime Harbour; river boat: Canary Wharf Pier*

Hampstead (O)

A particularly beautiful area located high above London. Winding streets with the houses of famous people: Keats House in Keats Grove; Fenton House in Hampstead Grove – a harpsichord on which Handel once played stands in this house; Grove Lodge in Admiral's Walk, the former residence of John Galsworthy, author of *The Forsyte Saga*. Nearby lies Hampstead Heath, a grassy expanse of park, woodland and lakes. Kenwood House, a charming Georgian mansion rebuilt in 1769 by the Scottish architect Robert Adam, is situated here. It has a beautiful Neoclassical façade; the house, with its important art collection, was bequeathed to the nation by the first Earl of Iveagh. Concerts are held by the lakeside in the summer, often ending in a final climax of fireworks. An ideal picnic spot is in front of Kenwood House with a view of the scenery, which has been immortalized by the paintings of J. Constable. No. 20 Maresfield Gardens was the home of Sigmund Freud and is now a museum. *Wed-Sun 12 pm–5 pm.* Tip: Hampstead Walks, an exploration on foot with an entertaining guide. *Tel: 0171-624 99 81; Underground: Hampstead*

Mayfair (110/C3)

Apart from Belgravia the most expensive residential area in London, but despite its luxurious Georgian elegance, it still retains some of its village character. A fair really did take place here every year in May until 1750. Nowadays it is an exclusive business address with shops in the upper price range. The old centre of Mayfair is Shepherd Market with winding lanes full of charm and known for its very discreet 'ladies'. Elizabeth II was born at 17 Bruton Street. Handel lived at 25 Brook Street for 30 years. 14 Savile Row: home to Hardy Amies, the Queen's couturier. The poet Lord Byron once lived in Albany Court. The Museum of Mankind in Burlington Gardens is well worth a visit. *Underground: Green Park*

Soho (103/E5)

Soho has a very cosmopolitan air, for it was here that the immigrants first arrived: Chinatown, the area between Gerrard, Lisle and Newport Streets, consists of countless Chinese restaurants, shops and video clubs. The Chinese New Year celebrations in February, which include six metre (20 foot) long 'dragons' and lots of noise, are very interesting. The different waves of Greek, French and Italian immigrants can still be seen in the variety of shops and restaurants in Soho. There are some very interesting theatres in Shaftesbury Avenue. Wardour, Greek, Frith and Dean Streets are today the mecca of the media industry: film distributors, agents, publishers — everyone who is anyone meets for coffee in the *Pâtisserie Valerie, 44 Old Compton Street,* and in cafés, bars and clubs such as the *O-Bar, 83–85 Wardour Street,* or *The Dog House, 187 Wardour Street.* Here and there a sex shop: Soho is also the red-light district of London. But this too is quite discreet — doorbells labelled only by a forename say everything. The buildings in Meard Street, which were former brothels, now cost £ 500,000!

Famous people in Soho: Mozart lived at 20 Frith Street when he was nine years old; Karl Marx lived with his family in a tiny flat at 28 Dean Street. Customers of the Italian restaurant *Quo Vadis* can view it. The painter Canaletto lived for 11 years at 41 Beak Street; his Venetian-tinged paintings of London are a reminder of this time. Charing Cross Road — on the edge of Soho and well known from old films — is the site of Foyles, the largest bookshop in London. The bookshops around Cecil Court are equally interesting. Modern Soho, with the latest fashions and stylish jewellery, can be found behind Liberty's on the other side of

Carnaby Street in Foubert's Place/ Marlborough Court/Newburgh Street. *Underground: Leicester Square/ Piccadilly*

Southall (O)

India in London! With all kinds of conceivable aromas and specialities. The salwar kamiz, the national costume of the Punjab, is the predominant fashion here, for this is where the majority of Punjabis from northern India live. Sikh temples, mosques and Hindu temples — people from the Indian subcontinent have been living in England since the 17th century. Gandhi, Nehru and many others studied in London. There is a total population of 400,000 Indians in London.

Shopping in Southall is absolutely fascinating: numerous shops selling presents, material, music and jewellery as well as precious silks and original Indian delicacies are to be found round about The Broadway and South Road. Curry has become just as 'British' as *chutney, cashmere* and *polo.* Try the *buttered chicken* in the *Brilliant, 72 Western Rd., Tel: 0181-574 19 28.* And please remember that the majority of Sikhs do not like being photographed. *British Rail: Southall; Underground: Hounslow West; then bus 232 to The Broadway*

HISTORIC HOUSES & PALACES

Dickens House (104/B3)

The novelist lived here from 1837 to 1839, when he wrote *Oliver Twist, Nicholas Nickleby* and *The Pickwick Papers.* Memorabilia, furniture and manuscripts. *Mon–Sat 10 am–5 pm; 48 Doughty Street; Underground: Russell Square*

Eton (O)

Eton College, the most famous public school in England, is situated about 50 minutes by train from London, near Windsor Castle. It was founded in 1440 by Henry VI as an apprentice's school. Worth seeing here are the school chapel, which contains wall paintings from the end of the 15th century, beautiful inner courtyards and cloisters, and the Eton boys (one of which is Prince William) in their tailcoat uniforms. School fees here are about £10,000 a year. *The church service on Sundays is open to the public; Tel: 01735-67 10 00; British Rail: from Waterloo to Windsor*

Hampton Court Palace (O)

★ A very popular destination in the vicinity of London, approximately half an hour by train from the centre of the city. Built of red brick and with tall decorated chimneys, this magnificent Tudor palace is set in extensive gardens and parkland by the River Thames. It looks particularly picturesque in spring. Built by Cardinal Wolsey in 1514, it was 'taken over' and developed by Henry VIII and later redesigned by Christopher Wren in Renaissance style. It is a microcosm of English architecture. George II completed the furnishings and added numerous paintings to the palace's important art collection, including works by Titian, Holbein and Van Dyck. Part of the palace was destroyed by fire in 1986; it is said that an occupant of the 'grace and favour' rooms, who are often the widows of deserving servants of the Crown, had been reading by candle light. The rooms have been completely restored and have been open to the public again since 1992. Take a look at the carvings by G. Gibbons. Outside the palace is Henry VIII's tennis court, the oldest maze in England and beautiful flower gardens as well as richly decorated wrought-iron gates down by the river. Since 1995, they have been part of the William III Park, which is identical to the original park from 1702. Five minutes' walk from here lies Bushey Park — with lots of tame deer. *Admission to State Apartments only. Park and grounds are free. British Rail: 25 minutes from Waterloo to Hampton Court*

Keats House (O)

★ The Romantic poet John Keats lived here from 1818 to 1820 in the loveliest part of Hampstead. This is where he wrote his 'Ode to a Nightingale', a love poem for his beloved Fanny. Manuscripts, memorabilia and furniture. *Mon–Fri 1 pm–5 pm; Nov-Apr 2 pm–6pm, Sat 10 am–1 pm, 2 pm–5 pm; Keats Grove; Underground: Belsize Park/Hampstead*

Leighton House (108/A–B2)

★ This house is crowded with collector's pieces, mostly from the Middle East. The exotic 'Arabian Hall' (complete with fountain) forms the centrepiece of an otherwise Victorian house. The hall is decorated with beautiful antique tiles, which Lord Leighton collected on his journeys to Damascus, Rhodes and Cairo. Directly beside Leighton House lies Holland Park, which contains a beautiful Japanese garden. *Mon–Sat 11 am–5 pm; 12 Holland Park Road; Underground: High Street Kensington*

Wellington Museum   (110/C2)

Formerly known as Apsley House or Number One London, this is the recently refurbished residence of the First Duke of Wellington, famous for his victory over Napoleon at Waterloo. It houses the Duke's noteworthy collection of paintings, sculptures, porcelain, silver, furniture, orders and decorations. *Tues–Sun 11 am–5 pm; Hyde Park Corner; Underground: Hyde Park Corner*

Windsor Castle   (O)

★ A must on every tourist's list – the largest inhabited castle in the world. It has been a residence of the English monarchs since the time of William the Conqueror and even today it is often used as a weekend retreat by the Windsors. The Royal Standard flies from the Round Tower when they are in residence. This tower is a typical feature of the Norman style in which Windsor Castle was built around 1300. It was developed into the present-day palace by George IV. St George's Chapel is one of the finest examples of the Perpendicular style in England. Don't miss Queen Mary's Dolls' House, an amazing dolls' house complete with electricity, water and a library. It is also worth standing in the queue to see the State Apartments (public reception rooms), in which state guests

are still received today. Former Soviet President Gorbatchev and former U.S. President Ronald Reagan dined here surrounded by the Queen's impressive art collection. Due to the fire of 1992, only 16 of the 18 rooms can be seen at present. *Mar–Nov 10 am–5 pm; Nov–Feb 10 am–4 pm; Admission Mon–Sat £8, Sun £5, family tickets are available. Long queues in the summer! British Rail: from Waterloo to Windsor*

PARKS

Crystal Palace   (O)

A park containing prehistoric monsters in plastic and lots of activities for children: boating on the lake, a children's zoo, a small funfair, nature trails. Famous athletes can often be seen training in the sports stadium. *Open daily from 7.30 am until dusk; British Rail: from Victoria to Crystal Palace*

Hyde Park   (109/D1–110/C2)

The largest of all the central London parks, Hyde Park, is 2 kilometres (1.2 miles) long and 900 metres (984 yards) wide. Although many of the old trees were destroyed in the storms of 1987 and 1990, the variety of trees and plants that is to be found here is still amazing. It is possible to go swimming or boating on 'The Serpentine', a shallow artificial lake, or enjoy just sitting in a deck chair! The Serpentine Gallery (Alexandra Gate) holds exhibitions of contemporary art. And not to be forgotten, of course: Speaker's Corner in the north-east corner of the park, famous for its 'soap box' orators on Sundays. *Underground: Hyde Park Corner/Lancaster Gate/Marble Arch (Speaker's Corner)*

Kensington Gardens (108/D2)
By crossing a little bridge you leave Hyde Park and enter Kensington Gardens. Thousands of daffodils bloom here in the spring! This is the site of the Albert Memorial and an exquisite statue designed by Sir George Frampton of Peter Pan, the fairy-tale figure created by J.M. Barrie. To the west lies Kensington Palace, the London residence of Prince Charles. The State Apartments are open to the public. The 'Court Dress Collection' which is kept here displays items worn at the British Courts from 1750 onwards. *Mon–Sat 9 am–5 pm, Sun 1 pm–5 pm; Underground: Queensway/Lancaster Gate*

Kew Gardens (O)
★ The 'Royal Botanic Gardens'. The leading botanic institution in the country cultivates more than 60,000 plant species and varieties on grounds covering an area of 120 hectares (300 acres). Some of England's most famous landscape gardeners contributed to its outlay: 'Capability' Brown, William Kent and Sir William Chambers. The Chinese Pagoda was designed by Sir William Chambers. The stars of Kew Gardens are the hot houses that date from the 19th century; the Temperate House is an ornately decorated Victorian cast-iron construction. Since 1990 about 1.6 million purple and white crocuses can be admired every spring, a gift from the *National Geographic.* There are marvellous displays of azaleas and rhododendrons. *Mar–Sept daily 9.30 am–6.30 pm; Sept–Nov daily 9.30 am–6 pm; Dec–Feb daily 9.30 am–4 pm; Admission: £3; Underground: Kew Gardens*

Regent's Park (102/A1–C3)
A smaller park designed by John Nash in 1812. Gleaming white Georgian terraced houses overlook the park. The English aristocracy has fulfilled its dream of a country house in the town here. In the centre of the park is a beautiful rose garden. Open-air performances of Shakespeare's plays take place in the theatre here in the summer. The park is also the site of the London Zoo, which was founded in 1826. *Underground: Baker Street/Regent's Park*

Richmond Park (O)
The largest of all the royal parks with an area of 660 hectares (1,630 acres), it is a lovely expanse of natural parkland. The 'Isabella Plantation', an area famous for its scented azaleas and rhododendrons, looks superb in all its tropical splendour in spring. Tame red and fallow deer have 'right of way' here: drivers of cars going through the woods wait patiently until the last deer has crossed the road. The Pen Ponds are small artificial lakes – a particular attraction for those interested in waterfowl. Ham House, a perfectly preserved country house dating from the 17th century, is approximately 15 minutes from the Ham Gate end of the park. Open daily until dusk. *Admission: £3; British Rail: Richmond; Underground: Rich-*

mond/Putney Bridge, then bus 71 to Richmond Hill

St James's Park (110–111/C–F2)

Much smaller than Hyde Park, but so idyllic that it should be combined with a visit to Buckingham Palace. Henry VIII had the marsh that was formerly here drained and converted the area into a deer park – Charles I crossed it on his way to his execution. Charles II commissioned the landscape gardener Le Nôtre, who had designed the gardens at Versailles for Louis XIV, with the transformation of the land into a formal garden. John Nash, architect to George IV, remodelled the result into a less formal, typically English landscape garden, with a lake full of ducks, wild geese and black swans. *Underground: St James's Park/Green Park/Charing Cross*

A visit to Madame Tussaud's

THE ROYAL FAMILY

The aura of the British monarchy fascinates tourists as well as Londoners. The Royal Family or 'the Firm': the Windsors are constantly under observation whether they are pursuing their hobbies, causing scandals or enjoying cultural events, but above all, of course, when they are taking part in the magnificent royal ceremonies. Annual highlights are the Opening of Parliament by the Queen and Trooping the Colour on the Queen's official birthday in June. However, there are many other occasions when there is lots to see for lovers of this kind of pageantry.

The ceremonial Changing of the Guard takes place every day outside Buckingham Palace at 11.30 am (every second day in winter). The Mounting of the Guard, performed by units of the royal *Household Cavalry,* can be watched on the parade grounds near Whitehall, *Horse Guards Parade, Mon–Sat 11 am, Sun 10 am.* It is also possible to see the guards in Hyde Park on their daily ride to their barracks. Part of Buckingham Palace is open to the public from 7 August to 1 October, *daily 9.30 am–5.30 pm.* Tickets are sold from nine o'clock; the entrance is on the St James's Park side of the palace. The private rooms are not on show. The Royal Mews: magnificent coaches and the most beautiful harness in the world (**111/D3**), *Wed and Thurs 2 pm–4 pm, Buckingham Palace Road.*

During the Royal Ascot race meeting, it is possible to see the Royal Family in the *royal enclo-*

sure, often only a few yards away from the 'people'. They also attend the Epsom Derby and the Horse Trials at Badminton. The opulence of royal lifestyle can be marvelled at in several shops, the 'purveyors to Her Majesty', i.e. the court suppliers, who also sell their goods to the general public.

Hampton Court Palace and Windsor Castle are, of course, both well worth a visit. Kensington Palace was the home of Diana, Princess of Wales. Countless bouquets of flowers were laid at its gates after her tragic death. The State Apartments, which include period furniture, works of art and ceremonial costumes, are open to the public. **(109/D1-2)** *Mon–Sat 9 am–5 pm; Admission: £2.60; Underground: Kensington High Street*

STREETS

Bond Street (102/C5)
Old Bond Street in particular is still classy — this is where Cartier, Asprey's, Gucci, expensive art galleries and antique shops as well as Sotheby's, the auction house, are all to be found. At the Oxford Street end: exclusive young fashions next to a very old-fashioned perfumery, such as Penhaligon's, which creates its own scents and sells them in beautiful old-fashioned bottles. *Underground: Bond Street*

Cheyne Row/Cheyne Walk (O)
The street with a special atmosphere in fashionable Chelsea: many extraordinary and highly individual houses dating from the 19th century when several famous writers, artists and scholars lived here. These included the painter William Turner (No. 118), the Pre-Raphaelite Dante Rossetti (No. 16), James Whistler, Henry James (No. 21), George Eliot (No. 4) and Thomas Carlyle (No. 24). Carlyle's house has been preserved in its original Victorian style and is now a museum. The Chelsea Physic Garden is the oldest botanic garden in London. Hundreds of rare plants and herbs can be seen here. Chelsea's most famous inhabitant must surely have been Oscar Wilde, who entertained the geniuses of his time in his home at 34 Tite Street, on the corner of Cheyne Place: Mallarmé, Yeats, Mark Twain and many others — including, of course, his friend Alfred Lord Douglas. Crosby Hall, part of a merchant's mansion from the 15th century, was moved here from Bishopsgate and now stands on the site of Thomas More's Chelsea garden. It has a beautifully carved oak roof, but unfortunately it is not open to the public. *Carlyle's House: Wed–Sun 11 am–5 pm; 24 Cheyne Row; Chelsea Physic Garden; Tel: 0171-352 56 46; from mid-Apr–end of Oct Wed and Sun 2 pm–5 pm; Underground: Sloane Square*

Fleet Street (104/C5)
For more than 200 years, this was the centre of London's newspaper industry. Many of the newspaper companies have now moved out to the Docklands, and their premises have been turned into offices. The former 'street of ink' is now better known for its old pubs, such as the wine bar *El Vino,* where

even today women in trousers are not served at the bar. *Underground: Blackfriars*

Hatton Garden (105/F4)

Not a garden, but a very unusual street. This was notorious as a very poor, run-down area in Dickens' time. Saffron Hill was immortalized by him in *Oliver Twist*. Today it is the centre of the jewellery trade in London. Countless jeweller's shops — yet not one stylish or elegant shop-window. Many orthodox Jews work here. In their traditional clothes, they are an unusual sight even in cosmopolitan London. *Underground: Farringdon*

Kensington High Street/Kensington Church Street (108/C3)

✠ Very popular shopping street for fashion and antiques. As well as expensive antique shops and smart restaurants there is also *Hyper Hyper*, a shopping paradise for the avant-garde, and *Kensington Market*, a covered market specializing in the latest in clothing. Very trendy! *Underground: High Street Kensington*

King's Road (110/A6)

✠ Famous in the '60s as a rendezvous of actors, artists and fashion designers. King's Road is *in* again, though more with the *trendies* who usually appear on Saturdays. At the end of the street, on Sloane Square, stands the Royal Court Theatre. It still maintains its reputation as a pioneer of the London theatre, specializing in experimental and innovative plays. The *sloane rangers*, yuppies with an inheritance who live in the Sloane Square area, are more likely to be in the wine bars and brasseries there. The *Oriel*, next to the Royal Court Theatre, is one of these. The streets running parallel to King's Road are also very interesting and worth taking some time to explore. At Brompton Cross, a new gourmet and design centre, beautifully decorated in Art Deco style, has been created in the old Michelin House. Here are restaurants and shops for people with good taste and lots of money. *Underground: Sloane Square*

Knightsbridge/Sloane Street (110/B3)

Knightsbridge, Brompton Road and Sloane Street: a very exclusive shopping district. At its centre are the department stores *Harrods* and *Harvey Nichols*. Boutiques for international *haute couture* as well as for modern British fashion can be found along Sloane Street. *The Scotch House* is recommended for high-quality knitwear, *Janet Reger* for super dessous at super prices, and *The General Trading Company* for fashions and presents. *Underground: Knightsbridge/South Kensington/Sloane Square*

Oxford Street (102–103/B6–F5)

Today a somewhat shabby, but popular shopping street with well-known addresses. Cheap fashion shops, a few good department stores, such as John Lewis. The vast *Virgin Superstore* is near the Tottenham Court Road Underground station. And near Marble Arch is *Selfridge's*, after Harrods the largest department store in London. *Underground: Marble Arch/Bond Street/Oxford Circus*

Pall Mall/St James's (111/F1)

Very elegant terraced houses designed by John Nash in the 19th century. Many of the exclusive gentlemen's clubs are situated here. (Women are sometimes tolerated as guests in these clubs but only in exceptional cases are they allowed to become members.) The Athenaeum Club in Waterloo Place is interesting: its façade is decorated with a copy of the Parthenon frieze. *Underground: Charing Cross*

Piccadilly (111/E1)

This lively shopping street runs from Piccadilly Circus to Hyde Park Corner. Here are some of the most elegant shops in London such as Simpson's and Fortnum & Mason, as well as the offices of a great many airlines and tourist boards. On the north side is Burlington House, home to the Royal Academy of Arts, which holds interesting exhibitions of modern and classical art. The famous Summer Exhibition is held here every year from May to August and promotes the works of contemporary British artists. Prince Charles exhibited his water-colours here anonymously. *Open daily 10 am–6 pm.* Next to it is the best shopping arcade in London for very stylish and expensive articles – the Burlington Arcade. Running parallel to Piccadilly is Jermyn Street, a shopping street for tailor-made shirts, perfumes and pot-pourris from *Floris* and the finest cheeses from the 18th century specialist cheesemonger *Paxton & Whitfield*. Further south beside the Ritz Hotel lies Green Park, which was once the hunting grounds of Charles II. It is now open for everyone to enjoy. Very colourful 'art exhibitions' are held along its railings at weekends. *Underground: Piccadilly Circus/Hyde Park Corner*

Regent Street (103/E6)

This bustling shopping street forms the dividing line between Mayfair and Soho. Regent Street is famous for its twinkling Christmas lights. At the Piccadilly end, there are elegant houses from the time of John Nash and some fascinating shops: the *court jeweller Garrard*, which designed the engagement rings of the Princess of Wales and the Duchess of York; *Hamleys*, the largest toy shop in the world; and *Liberty's*, which is famous for its fabrics and silk scarves. Just around the corner is Carnaby Street, which is beginning to recover some of its earlier popularity. If you explore some of the side streets here, you will find tiny shops with the very latest fashions as well as alternative restaurants. *Underground: Piccadilly Circus/Oxford Circus*

Shaftesbury Avenue (103/F6)

This was formerly the centre of theatreland in London. Owing to economic pressures, the old theatres that have survived here are very commercially oriented, but they are still worth visiting, even if only for their decor! The famous 'Les Misérables' – nicknamed 'The Glums' – is on at the Palace Theatre; 'The Phantom of the Opera' can be seen not far away in Haymarket. *Underground: Piccadilly Circus*

Whitehall/
Downing Street (112/A1)

This street of impressive Neoclassical buildings extends from Westminster Bridge to Trafalgar Square. This was formerly the site of the vast royal Palace of Whitehall, which stretched from the Thames to St James's. A fire destroyed most of it in 1698, but the Banqueting House survived. Today it houses the 'corridors of power': the Civil Service has its headquarters here and in Westminster. No. 10 Downing Street has been the official residence of the British Prime Minister since 1732 and No. 11, immediately beside it, is the official residence of the Chancellor of the Exchequer. *Underground: Westminster*

SQUARES

Berkeley Square (111/D1)

One of the best business addresses in London. This is where the annual debutante ball for *sloanes* (members of the rich middle class) takes place in a marquee: *Admission £150 per person; Underground: Bond Street/Green Park*

The Boltons (109/D5)

Its distance from the Underground is significant: this has always been where people with a chauffeur have lived. Beautiful and well worth the walk. *Between Brompton Road and Gilston Road; Underground: Gloucester Road*

Cornwall Gardens (109/D4)

Lovely Neoclassical houses and old trees — it is well worth exploring the neighbourhood. *Underground: Gloucester Road*

Eaton Square (110/C4)

Elegant residential area (Belgravia). Stylish boutiques in the side streets. *Underground: Sloane Square*

Old Square/New Square (104/B3)

Two lovely tranquil squares that are part of the grounds of Lincoln's Inn, one of the Inns of Court. New Square is the only square in London that has been completely preserved from the 17th century. Immediately adjacent are Lincoln's Inn Fields — the largest 'square' in London. *Underground: Chancery Lane*

Piccadilly Circus (111/F1)

At the very centre of London's entertainment world. Piccadilly Circus has been renovated over the past few years; for many it is at its best when lit up at night by huge advertising signs. *Underground: Piccadilly Circus*

Soho Square (103/F5)

A peaceful little green area five minutes away from bustling Oxford Street — a rendezvous for the 'media people' who work in Soho. *Underground: Tottenham Court Road*

Trafalgar Square (112/A1)

This is where all the tourists — and the pigeons — congregate. The Royal Mews were located here when the Palace of Whitehall was the main royal residence. The present-day square was created in 1830. Nelson Column, 44 m (145 ft) high and erected to honor the hero of the Battle of Trafalgar, is one of London's most famous landmarks, although the fountains are more popular in summer. *Underground: Charing Cross*

Two hours in a museum

Treasures from all over the world are on display in the showcases of London's museums, such as the Elgin Marbles in the British Museum

Nowhere else in the world are there so many and such diverse and impressive collections as here in London, *the* museum capital of the world. London visitors benefit from the former extent of the British Empire. Everything is here from the antiquity to the Apollo capsule. Museums are a good place to go when it rains and admission to many of the museums and art galleries is even free. Reductions are available for some museums with the 'White Card'. *(Tel: 0171-923 08 07; Fax: 249 03 96, available by post or at the museums).* All museums are closed from 24 to 28 December, as well as on 1 January, Good Friday and 1 May.

Bethnal Green Museum of Childhood (O)

This building, constructed of iron and glass in 1872, houses the largest collection of toys in Britain.

The Neoclassical façade of the Tate Gallery, which houses the works of William Turner as well as modern masterpieces

Mon–Thurs, Sat 10 am–5.50 pm, Sun 2.30 pm–5.50 pm; Cambridge Heath Road; Underground: Bethnal Green

British Museum (104/A4)

★ The British Museum is one of the most famous museums in the world and has 5.9 million visitors every year. It houses priceless collections of Egyptian, Greek and Roman antiques, finds from excavations in Assyria and Babylonia, art from south and south east Asia, China and the European Middle Ages. There is so much to see that visitors must restrict themselves to a number of specific exhibits. The Elgin Marbles, for example, the sculptures and friezes from the Parthenon in Athens, which Lord Elgin 'imported' in 1803, should not be missed. The Duveen Gallery, a high, light room with displays of marble friezes, is breathtaking (Room 8). An exceptional showpiece is the Rosetta Stone in Room 25, which enabled scholars to decipher Egyptian hieroglyphic writing after 4,000 years – a comparison of the inscriptions in three different languages made this possible. Don't miss the Egyptian Collection: Rooms 60–64 have abundant displays of mummies. Take a look at the British Library Reading Room: its dome has a diameter of 47 m (155 ft), which means that it is larger than the dome of St Peter's Cathedral in Rome. This is where Karl Marx, Sigmund Freud, Lenin, Charles Dickens and George Bernard Shaw read and wrote their works. The 'copyright privilege' means that a copy of every book published in Great Britain has to be donated to the library, which has amassed a collection of more than 10 million volumes from 1757 to the present day. Tours begin every hour on the hour. *Mon–Sat 10 am–5 pm, Sun 2.30 pm–6 pm, guided tours last 90 minutes, tours of the Reading Room are given hourly, 11 am–4 pm; Great Russell Street; Underground: Russell Square/Holborn/Tottenham Court Road*

Commonwealth Experience (108/B3)
Here you can gain an impression of the vast range of influence of Victorian Britain. Information on all Commonwealth countries, a well-stocked library, exhibitions and an art gallery. Also included are a cinema and a restaurant. Behind it lies Holland Park, which is a mass of roses in the summer! *Mon–Sat 10 am–5 pm, Sun 2.30 pm–6 pm; Kensington High Street; Underground: High Street Kensington*

Cutty Sark (O)
For ship lovers: the Cutty Sark was the fastest and most famous of the British tea-clippers, which brought tea to England from

China in the 19th century. Close by is berthed Gypsy Moth IV, the little yacht in which Sir Francis Chichester sailed single-handed round the world in 1966–67. Nearby: National Maritime Museum, Royal Observatory, Royal Naval College. *Mon–Sat 10 am–5 pm, Sun 11 am–5 pm; King William Walk, Greenwich; British Rail: Maze Hill; river boat: from Westminster and Tower Pier; Docklands Light Railway: from Tower Gate to Island Gardens then walk through the tunnel under the Thames to Greenwich*

Design Museum (114/B2)
★ Opened in 1989 as the first museum in the world for the contemporary design of mass-produced goods. The collection explains the form and function of everyday things. The museum was built as part of the 'Butler's Wharf Development', the conversion of old warehouses in the former Docklands east of Tower Bridge. There are several other places in the vicinity worth visiting, e. g. the *Bramah Tea & Coffee Museum* or *Hay's Galleria*, a small new shopping centre. *Tues–Sun 11.30 am–6.30 pm; Butler's Wharf, Shad Thames; Underground: Tower Hill/London Bridge; river boat: London Bridge City*

Geological Museum (109/F4)
One of the world's leading earth science museums. The numerous objects on display are clearly marked and presented. There are extensive collections of gems, fossils, rocks and minerals. The exhibition includes a very interesting audio-visual presentation of the earth's history. *Mon–Sat 10 am–6 pm, Sun 2.30 pm–6 pm;*

Exhibition Road; Underground: South Kensington

Institute of Contemporary Art (ICA) (111/E2)

Hidden behind the elegant Carlton House Terrace is the ICA, an 'adults' playground'. Cinema, ballet, drama, all the performing arts and contemporary exhibitions are to be found here. There is also a good snack bar. For a small fee you can become a member — even just for one day —of the ICA, a private club of devotees of the latest in art. *Daily 12 pm–1 am; The Mall; Underground: Piccadilly Circus/Charing Cross*

Jewish Museum (O)

The Jewish Museum displays an interesting collection of Jewish antiques and ritual objects. Immediately adjacent to it is the Jewish Cultural Centre. *Mon–Thurs 10 am–4 pm; 129 Albert Street; Underground: Camden Town*

Kew Bridge Steam Museum (O)

This museum houses the largest collection in the world of working steam engines, monsters of 19th century technology. Note: the machines are only in operation at weekends! *Daily 11 am–5 pm; Green Dragon Lane, Brentford, Middlesex; British Rail: from Waterloo to Kew Bridge*

London Dungeon Museum (113/F1)

Horror museum which shows visitors the most gruesome and cruel episodes in the history of

---

MARCO POLO SELECTION: MUSEUMS

1 British Museum
The Elgin Marbles enchant every visitor (pages 39–40)

2 Design Museum
The 20th century reflected in mass-produced consumer goods, (page 40)

3 Imperial War Museum
'Blitz Experience' – the horrors of war (page 45)

4 MOMI
Interactive museum – a must for film fans (page 42)

5 National Gallery
Gainsborough – the essence of 18th-century British painting (page 42)

6 Natural History Museum
Natural history brought to life (pages 42–43)

7 Museum of London
The Lord Mayor of London's golden coach (page 42)

8 Tate Gallery
Home of the Turner Collection (page 43)

9 Victoria & Albert Museum
The Jones Collection: Europe in the 18th century – tasteful furnishings cleverly presented (pages 43–44)

England from the Middle Ages to the 17th century. Scenes of death, torture and burning martyrs at the stake. Tour lasts two hours. *Daily 10 am–5.30 pm, Oct–Mar 10 am–4.30 pm; 28–34 Tooley Street; Underground: London Bridge*

Madame Tussaud's/ Planetarium (102/B4)

The sum of £10 million has been spent on redesigning the most famous waxworks museum in the world. Now you go on a journey by 'time taxi' through the last 400 years of London's history – past moving figures and scenes complete with sounds and smells. *Avoid the queues by booking in advance. Tel: 0171-935 68 61; Fax: 465 08 62; Mon–Fri 10 am–5.30 pm, Sat, Sun 9.30 am–5.30 pm; Planetarium shows every 40 mins from 12.30 pm to 5 pm; Marylebone Road; Underground: Baker Street*

Museum of London (105/E4)

★ Illustrates the history of London from prehistoric times to the present day. Very successful presentations of social and domestic life in the capital. It features an audio-visual display of the Great Fire of London, which destroyed most of the city in 1666. *Tues-Sat 10 am–6 pm, Sun 12 pm–6 pm; London Wall; Underground: Barbican/St Paul's/Moorgate*

Museum of the Moving Image (MOMI) (112/B1)

★ This museum of 'moving pictures' entertainingly illustrates the development of cinema and TV. *Daily 10 am–6 pm, last admission 5 pm; South Bank Centre; Underground: Waterloo*

National Gallery (112/A1)

★ The National Gallery is one of the most important art galleries in the world. It possesses more than 4,500 works of art, of which 2,000 are on show at any one time. The gallery includes masterpieces from all major European schools and periods; the collection of Dutch paintings and of the 15th- and 16th-century Italian schools are some of the most valuable. For those who are pressed for time, a leaflet is available at the Information Desk detailing a short tour that takes in some of the most famous masterpieces. Don't miss Rembrandt's *Self-Portrait* (Room 27), Leonardo da Vinci's cardboard drawing *The Virgin and Child* (lower floor), Hans Holbein the Younger's *The Ambassadors* (Room 5), the collection of French Impressionist paintings (Rooms 43–45), especially Monet's *Water Lilies* (Room 46) and Redon's *Ophelia* (Room 45). Works by Constable and Gainsborough are in Room 34. *Mon–Sat 10 am–6 pm, Sun 2 pm–6 pm, July–Sept Wed 10 am–8 pm; Trafalgar Square; Underground: Charing Cross*

Natural History Museum (109/F4)

★ The museum is housed in a vast and elaborate neo-Romanesque/Byzantine-style building which despite its length of 230 metres (760 feet) still gives an impression of classical lightness. The collections contain 40 million objects: huge dinosaur skeletons, insects, fossils, plants and animals. The skeleton of a 30 metre (100 foot) blue whale can be seen here. Since the amalgamation of the museum with the Geological Museum, it possesses the most extensive meteorite collection in the world. The 'Earth Galleries' include audio-visual shows on the history of the earth. *Free admission from 5 pm until 5.50 pm, Mon–Sat 10 am–6 pm, Sun 2.30 pm–6 pm; Cromwell Road; Underground: South Kensington*

Old Royal Observatory (O)

The Observatory is located in Greenwich Park overlooking the River Thames. It was commissioned by Charles II for John Flamsteed, the first royal astronomer, and was built in 1675 by Christopher Wren. The prime meridian of the world runs through the middle of the former observatory. This is also where 'Greenwich Mean Time' (GMT) was determined. At the entrance is the 24-hour clock, which lets a red timeball fall every day precisely at 1 pm – and has done since 1833! Next to the Old Royal Observatory is the National Maritime Museum. *Mar–Oct Mon–Sat 10 am–6 pm, Sun 2 pm–6 pm; Nov–Mar Sat 10 am–5 pm, Sun 2 pm–5 pm; British Rail: Maze Hill; by boat to Greenwich Pier; Docklands Light Railway: from Tower Gateway to Island Gardens, then walk through the tunnel under the Thames to Greenwich*

Science Museum (109/F4)

The wonders of technology are displayed on five floors in the Science Museum in an easily understandable and entertaining way. These include the oldest surviving steam locomotive 'Puffing Billy' (1813) in the Boiler House, veteran cars, a submarine and the Apollo 10 command module (Gallery 6). Exhibits on the exploration of space and the development of computers. Interactive children's galleries. *Mon–Sat 10 am–6 pm, Sun 11 am–6 pm; Exhibition Road; Underground: South Kensington*

Tate Gallery (112/A5)

★ The gallery houses two national collections. The British Collection covers the period 1500 to 1900; Hogarth, Blake, Stubbs, Constable and the Pre-Raphaelites are particularly stongly represented. The 20th-Century Collection includes paintings and sculpture by British artists after 1860 and by foreign artists from the Impressionists onwards. The Tate Gallery is renowned for its modern works of art, some of which have aroused great controversy. The Clore Gallery houses the works of William Turner, which he left to the nation on his death. The gallery was completely reorganized in 1990: a constantly changing display is supposed to emphasize the unpredictable importance of all works of art. Particularly noteworthy in the 20th-Century Collection: the Mark Rothko gallery (Gallery 28). Be sure not to miss: Lucian Freud's *Standing by the Rags*, Auguste Rodin's *The Kiss*, Max Ernst's *Celebes*, works by Anselm Kiefer and Joseph Beuys. *Mon–Sat 10 am–6 pm, Sun 2 pm–6 pm; Millbank; Underground: Pimlico*

Victoria & Albert Museum (109/F4)

★ The V & A was opened in 1909 as the 'National Museum of Fine and Applied Art'. Here are displays of art, furniture, fabrics, silver, glass, ceramics and jewellery in almost 150 rooms. It is best to select a few exhibits of particular interest from this vast collection. Go through the side entrance in Exhibition Road to the Henry Cole Wing. On level 6 there is an excellent collection of paintings by John Constable – there is also a marvellous view over London from here! On the Lower Ground Floor is a gallery which in itself makes a visit here worthwhile: the Jones Collection. Furniture, paintings, porcelain, mostly European objects dating from the 18th century, have been combined to form complete rooms (Galleries 1–7). Delicate porcelain from Dresden and a lovely secretaire made by Boulle for Louis XIV can be seen here (Room 5). Imagine that you are Madame de Serilly in her beautiful boudoir (Room 7). Then return to the main entrance, where it is difficult to decide where to go next: perhaps the world famous Raphael cartoons (Room 48). The Dress Collection, the most important collection of period clothes in the world (Room 40). Glittering crystal in the new Glass Gallery (Room 130). For Rodin fans: the largest collection of his sculptures, outside Paris (Room 21)! For lovers of ceramic: Rooms 127 and 128. For Art Nouveau fans: an exhibition on William Morris, the founder of the 'Arts and Crafts' Movement (Room 13), and the marvellously tiled Poynter & Gamble Rooms (Rooms 14 and 15). For lovers of the Italian art: the most famous collection of Italian sculpture outside Italy (Rooms 11, 13, 15). *Mon–Thurs, Sat 10 am–5.30 pm,*

Cromwell Road; Underground: South Kensington

Wallace Collection (102/C5)

This collection is housed in an elegant town house built for the Duke of Manchester in 1776, which lies behind busy Oxford Street. Rare treasures have been amassed here: French Sèvres porcelain and 18th-century painting as well as furniture, in particular Renaissance pieces, can all be admired here. Room 19 is the most important, with works by Rembrandt, Rubens, Murillo, Gainsborough, Velázquez and Van Dyck. And Frans Hals's *Laughing Cavalier. Mon–Sat 10 am–5 pm, Sun 2 pm–5 pm; Hertford House/Manchester Square; Underground: Bond Street*

MILITARY MUSEUMS

World War I and II remain a very popular topic, discussed amongst a large section of the English population. This is prob-

Victoria & Albert Museum

ably due to the many films and documentaries of varying quality so often broadcast on television. Exellent war movies made for the big screen, featuring popular actors, also help the general public not to forget the cruel, unnecessary horrors of war. The documentary 'The World at War' comes to mind.

Unfortunately mankind has, and always will have a tendency to wage wars against one another and London has many great museums where one can reflect and see those interesting times of our history.

Britain at War Experience (113/F1)

High-tech methods depict the life of the civilian population in London during the Blitz of 1940/41. *Oct–Mar daily 10 am–4.30 pm, Apr–Sept 10 am–5.30 pm; 64/66 Tooley Street; Underground: London Bridge*

Cabinet War Rooms (112/A2)

A vast labyrinth of underground rooms and passages where Churchill held his Cabinet meetings and spoke to the nation on the radio during World War II Everything is preserved as it was in the '40s, even the gas masks are still hanging on their hooks. *Daily 10 am–5 pm; Clive Steps, King Charles Street; Underground: Westminster*

Chislehurst Caves (O)

These enormous chalk caves are about 8,000 years old, and stretch for a length of 25 kilometres (15 miles) underneath the county of Kent. Druids, Saxons and Romans have all left their individual traces here. In World War II the caves were used to house 15,000 people: an air-raid shelter with a hospital, sleeping quarters, canteens, a cinema, a dance hall and shops. *Easter–Sept daily 11am–5 pm; Sept–Easter Sat/Sun 11 am–5 pm; phone to book a guided tour: Tel: 0181-467 32 61; Caveside Close, Old Hill; British Rail: from Waterloo to Chislehurst station, approx. 25 minutes*

HMS Belfast (112/B1)

A Royal Navy cruiser, one of the last big-gun warships, now a floating museum. All seven decks are open to visitors, from the bridge to the boiler rooms. Nearby: Hay's Galleria; Butler's Wharf. *Mar–Oct daily 11 am–5.30 pm, Nov–Feb 11 am–5 pm; Symons Wharf, Vine Lane, Tooley Street; or with the ferry from Tower Pier; Tel: 0171-407 64 34; Underground: London Bridge*

Imperial War Museum (113/E4)

★ The museum was founded in 1920, shortly after World War I and it traces the history of the two World Wars and other British and Commonwealth military operations since 1914. The collection includes 9,000 pictures, weapons, uniforms, decorations, military vehicles and aircraft (the Spitfire is not to be missed). There are battle ships from World War I as well as Hitler's last will and exhibitions on the fighting in Lebanon and Burma. Audio-visual effects simulate the German air raids over London in the 'Blitz Experience'. *Mon–Sat 10am–5.50 pm, Sun 2 pm–5.50 pm; Lambeth Road; Underground: Lambeth North/Elephant & Castle*

Where to dine

International cuisine:
the best and most unusual restaurants in London

One of the most pleasant surprises for the foreign visitor to London is the new British cuisine. London has become Europe's most exciting culinary capital. Dishes from more than 100 different countries can be sampled here. And most interesting of all are the new developments in traditional British cooking, enriched by the influence of all the immigrants over the past fifty years. English food, however, can be quite expensive. Ethnic cuisines provide a good alternative, especially the many Chinese and Indian restaurants, Italian restaurants such as 'Pizza Express', the 'Bella Pasta' or 'Café Rouge' chains, or 'Cranks', a chain of vegetarian restaurants. Or you can order a fixed-price menu, which means that your complete meal is covered by a set price. In expensive restaurants these menus are normally only available at lunch time. Bear in mind that prices do not always include the

Old English restaurants are just as nice inside as they are from the outside

service charge and VAT. If a service charge is not included, leave a tip of about 15% of the bill. You can also have a good, substantial meal at a reasonable price in the carveries of some hotels. Here the chef cuts as much as you want from enormous tasty joints of beef, lamb and pork. Or try a sandwich at lunch time, e.g. in the *Aurora Café, 49 Lexington Street.* If you really have no idea where to go for a meal, ring the Restaurant Switchboard: tell them what you would like and how much you are willing to spend and they will advise you – and this service is free! *Mon–Sat 9 am–7 pm, Tel: 0181-888 80 80.*

Do remember that very few restaurants in London are open on Sundays. Restaurants are normally open from 12 pm until 3 pm and from 7 pm until 11 pm; brasseries are often open all day.

In England most people usually eat their main meal in the evening and just have a snack at lunchtime. A full traditional breakfast is often only eaten at weekends. In many hotels an extra charge is made for an English breakfast.

MARCO POLO SELECTION: RESTAURANTS

1 The Blue Elephant
Exotic ambience, delicious Thai cuisine (pages 51–52)

2 Thomas Goodes
Extraordinary teas, interior and prices (page 49)

3 Café Delancey
France in the middle of Camden (page 54)

4 Chuen Cheng Ku
Tasty snacks – dim-sum specialists (page 52)

5 Oxo Tower
Super view of the Thames and Big Ben from the bar (page 51)

6 Quaglino's
Large and most elegant restaurant (page 51)

7 Rudland & Stubbs
Old-fashioned fish restaurant in the middle of the meat market (page 49)

8 Rani
Finest vegetarian cuisine from India (page 53)

9 Rules
Traditional elegance from the turn of the century (page 49)

10 Sweetings
Really old and very popular fish restaurant famous for it's oysters (page 50)

The eating order of a traditional dinner is normally as follows: a small starter of sorts (often soup); – the main coarse and then the all important dessert which regularly includes a slice of cake or two. An appertizer is usually called for after dinner and may consist of a gin and tonic (very popular) or a sherry. Others may prefer a cognac or a good port wine with a cup of coffee to help digest the meal.

We have classified the restaurants in this guide in four categories, which refer to the price of a meal with wine for one person. The budget-priced restaurants are in *category 3* (up to £ 15 for a meal), medium-priced restaurants are in *category 2* (£ 15 to £ 25 for a meal), more expensive restaurants in *category 1* (£ 25 to £ 50 for a meal), and top-quality restaurants are in *category L* (more than £ 50 for a meal). At the end of this chapter we have included a selection of wine bars and brasseries, where you can also have an excellent and often economical meal at realistic prices. Pubs are not included in this section. Since drinking is of more importance than eating there, they are included in the chapter on entertainment.

AFTERNOON TEA

A really traditional English afternoon tea consists of dainty salmon, cheese or cucumber sandwiches, cakes and scones with strawberry jam and cream. 'Nothing wrong with a jolly cup of tea, what?'

Café Nero (103/F5)

A new café in the chic area of Soho – directly opposite the popular old bar, Italia. *Category 3; 66 Old Compton Street; Underground: Leicester Square*

Café de Paris (103/F6)

On Sundays a tea dance is held in this elegant and completely refurbished club from the turn of the century. *Category 2; 3 pm – 6.30 pm; £ 12; Tel: 0171-734 77 00; 3 Coventry Street; Underground: Piccadilly*

Palm Court (104/B5)

Traditional afternoon tea in the café of the Ritz Hotel. Men must be dressed semi-formaly; just a jacket or jeans and a pullover are not acceptable. *Category L; Piccadilly; Tel: 0171-493 81 81; Underground: Green Park*

Thomas Goodes (102/C5)

★Not only the tea but also the china is exquisite here – a set costs£ 1,500! *Category L; from 4 pm; 19 South Audley Street; Underground: Green Park/Bond Street*

ENGLISH CUISINE

Aunties (103/E5)

Lamb chops with mint sauce, crab soup, mussels, trifle. Family photographs on green walls, black and white tiles. Furnished with what some might label traditional genuine English Edwardian fixtures. British wines. *Category 1; 126 Great Portland Street; Tel: 0171-387 32 26; Underground: Warren Street*

The Bluebird (110/B5)

The latest successful experiment from the restaurant guru Sir Terence Conran. Good nouvelle cuisine with seating for 240 people. Next to it is a shopping paradise for lovers of Tuscany. *Category 1; 350 King's Road; Tel: 0171-559 10 00; Underground: Sloane Square*

Le Caprice (111/E1)

New British cuisine is perfectly prepared and charmingly served here – rendezvous for the smart set without the stiff British upper lip. *Category 3; Arlington House, Arlington Street; Tel: 0171-629 22 39; Underground: Green Park*

The Hope and Sirloin (105/D4)

You can have a typical English breakfast here – instead of lunch. *Category 3; 94 Cowcross Street; Tel: 0171-253 85 25; Underground: Farringdon*

Rudland & Stubbs (105/D4)

★ This fish restaurant is located in the middle of Smithfield meat market. Spit and sawdust: very simple interior. But there is a large selection: oyster bar, fish-cakes. Children welcome. *Category 2; 35–37 Greenhill's Rents, Crowcross Street; Tel: 0171-253 01 48; Underground: Farringdon*

Rules (104/A6)

★ This is supposedly the oldest restaurant in London (1798), which means that it's been around for a while and therefore not exactly cheap. Famous for its traditional specialities and game: jugged hare or calf's liver with onions and bacon. Popular with the English aristocracy and also artists. Open all day. *Category 1; 35 Maiden Lane; Tel: 0171-836 53 14; Underground: Covent Garden*

Chinese cuisine on two floors at the Chuen Cheng Ku

Sea Shell Fish Restaurant (102/B3)
This establishment offers superior fish and chips. It's somewhat expensive, but the portions are simply enormous and of the highest quality. A large, friendly restaurant, − Take away, too. *Category 2; 49 Lisson Grove; Tel: 0171-723 87 03; Underground: Marylebone*

Sweetings (105/F5)
★ This really old restaurant has hardly changed since it was established in 1830. Famous for its Colchester oysters and its fish dishes. Especially delicious: smoked shellfish with eggs, herring roe on toast. 'City' clientele. only open at lunch time. It is best to be there at 12 o'clock, since tables cannot be reserved and it is always filled to capacity. *Category 1; 39 Queen Victoria Street; Tel:0171-248 30 62 Underground: Bank*

Tiddy Dols Eating House (110/C1)
Tiny interconnecting houses in the centre of Mayfair. Old English 'cabaret' every evening, lute players. On the menu: beef Wellington, shepherd's pie, roast beef, Tiddy Dol chicken. Children welcome. *Category 2; 55 Shepherd Market, Mayfair; Tel: 0171-499 23 57; Underground: Green Park*

The Wig and Pen (104/C6)
Formerly a club for lawyers and journalists, now a restaurant that serves traditional food, such as bangers and mash or liver and bacon. *Category 2; The Strand; Tel: 0171-353 33 44; Underground: Temple*

RESTAURANTS WITH A GARDEN

Belvedere (108/B3)
Situated in an idyllic location in Holland Park. The atmosphere is smart but casual. Modern British cuisine. *Category 1; Holland House, Holland Park, entrance Abbotsbury-Melbury Road; Tel: 0171-602 12 38; Underground: Kensington High Street/Holland Park*

Frederick's (105/D1)
Very popular with visitors of the Camden Passage antique market. Large conservatory. Varied menu. Highly recommended: stuffed chicken. *Category 1; Camden Passage; Tel: 0171-359 28 88; Underground: Angel*

Henry J. Beans (110/B5)
Tex-mex, spare ribs, hamburgers, salads – in a large garden in the King's Road. Relaxed atmosphere. *Category 2; 195 King's Road; Tel: 0171-352 92 55; Underground: Sloane Square*

The Sugar Club (100/C5)

Small but friendly restaurant in the smart Ledbury Road area. Old rock stars such as Mick Jagger and young media stars dine here and can no doubt recommend the lamb chops with mushrooms and lentils. *Category 2; 33 a All Saint's Road; Tel: 0171-221 38 44; Underground: Westbourne Park*

UNUSUAL RESTAURANTS

Alfred (103/E6)

Good cocktails, consistently good traditional and new British food such as bubble & squeak and lemon tart. *Category 3; 245 Shaftesbury Avenue; Tel: 0171-240 25 66; Underground: Covent Garden*

Blueprint Café (114/C2)

Located in the Design Museum but also open to those not visiting the museum. Lovely view of the Tower Bridge. *Category 2; Shad Thames; Tel: 0171-378 70 31; Underground: Tower Hill*

Down Mexico Way (103/F6)

Super atmosphere: salsa, lambada dancers. Good steaks, fajitas. *Category 3; bar 7 pm–3 am, Sun until 10.30 pm; 25 Swallow Street; Tel: 0171-437 98 95; Underground: Piccadilly Circus*

First Floor (100/A5)

Directly adjacent to the equally fashionable Market Bar, daring Italian and new British cuisine. Young clientele, smart but casual. *Category 1; Portobello Road; Tel: 0171-243 00 72; Underground: Ladbroke Grove*

The Lebanese Restaurant (102/A5)

Finest Lebanese food. Highly recommended: the oriental starters, mezze. *Category 2; 60 Edgware Road; Tel: 0171-723 91 30; Underground: Marble Arch*

Livebait (112/C2)

Old-fashioned fish restaurant not far from Waterloo and the South Bank Centre. *Category 1; 43 The Cut; Tel: 0171-928 72 11; Underground: Waterloo*

Mezzo (103/E5)

One of the largest restaurants in London, seats 700. Friendly, lively and trendy. *Category 2; 100 Wardour Street; Tel: 0171-314 40 00; Underground: Piccadilly Circus*

Oxo Tower (112/C1)

★ Smart new restaurant by the Thames, on the eighth floor with a marvellous view of Big Ben – which can also be seen from the bar. *Category 1; Barge House Street South Bank; Tel: 0171-803 38 38; Underground: Waterloo*

Quaglino's (110/D2)

★ The largest and most elegant restaurant in London, it can be compared with 'La Coupole' in Paris. Quag's specialities: seafood, grilled lamb. Consistently good, lots of glamour. Advance booking is essential here! *Category 2; jazz from 11 pm; 16 Bury Street; Tel: 0171-930 67 67; Underground: Green Park*

ASIAN RESTAURANTS

The Blue Elephant (O)

★ Fantastic oriental decor with numerous plants. Good Thai food. An experience! *Category L; 4–6 Fulham Broadway; Tel: 0171-*

385 65 95; Underground: Fulham Broadway

Chuen Cheng Ku (103/F6)

★ Vast restaurant on two floors. The menu includes prawn in rice paper and barbecued duck as well as delicious dim-sum dishes. The latter are only available at lunch time and are served from a trolley beside your table. *Category 2; 17 Wardour Street; Tel: 0171-437 13 98; Underground: Piccadilly*

Ikkyu (103/E4)

A reasonably priced Japanese basement café. Very popular. *Category 3; 67 Tottenham Court Road; Tel: 0171-436 61 69; Underground: Goodge Street*

Krungtap 9 (108/C6)

Original Thai cuisine. Friendly service, unfortunately only open in the evenings from 5 pm. *Category 2; Old Brompton Road; Tel: 0171-259 23 14; Underground: Earl's Court*

GOURMET RESTAURANTS IN LONDON

Bibendum (109/F5)

Classical French cuisine in latest English style in an Art Deco palace. From £75. *Open daily (except Sun); 81 Fulham Road; Tel: 0171-581 58 17; Underground: South Kensington*

The Café Royal (111/F1)

Grill room. This beautiful Baroque room has at last got a chef who earns his Michelin star! From £45. *Open daily (except Sun), no lunch Sat, 12.30 pm–2.30 pm, 7 pm–10.30 pm; 68 Regent Street; Tel: 0171-437 90 90; Underground: Piccadilly Circus*

Tante Claire (110/B5)

Pierre Kaufmann has been serving the best French cuisine here for years, a restaurant for those who expect the highest quality. Especially delicious: duck or pig's trotters stuffed with mushrooms! Dignified and friendly atmosphere. £50 for set lunch, otherwise more expensive. *68 Royal Hospital Road; Tel: 0171-352 60 47; Underground: Sloane Square*

Le Gavroche (102/B6)

Founder of the modern British *haute cuisine*. Caloric ecstasy in discreetly luxurious surroundings. The food here has been consistently good for years, which is also true of the – cheaper – brasserie. 3 Michelin stars. From £75. *43 Upper Brook Street; Tel: 0171-408 0881; Underground: Marble Arch*

Restaurant Marco-Pierre White (101/F1)

England's most successful young chef White celebrates his art in the luxury hotel Meridien Piccadilly. From £100. *Piccadilly; Tel and Fax: 0171-734 80 00; Underground: Piccadilly*

Ritz (101/E1)

The most famous hotel restaurant in the world. Louis XVI decor, gold, marble, mirrors and paintings. A great experience: dinner dance and cabaret on Fridays and Saturdays. From £60. *Open daily; Piccadilly; Tel:0171-493 81 81; Underground: Green Park*

Mandarin Kitchen (101/D6)
The best Asian seafood outside Soho: prawns with ginger, lobster in black bean sauce. *Category 2; 14–16 Queensway; Tel: 0171-727 90 12; Underground: Piccadilly Circus*

Satay Stick (103/D5)
Malaysian cooking, not far from Oxford Street, good and reasonably priced. *Category 3; 6 Dering Street; Tel: 0171-629 13 46; Underground: Bond Street*

Suntory (111/E2)
The best and most expensive Japanese restaurant, wonderful sushi. *Set lunch. Category L; 72–73 St James's Street; Tel: 0171-409 02 01; Underground: Green Park*

The Tamarind (101/D1)
Luxurious restaurant in Mayfair – but a special menu at lunchtime for £18.50 gives you the chance to sample modern Indian cooking at a fairly good price. Specially recommended: kakori kebabs. *Category 1; 20 Queens Street; Tel: 0171-629 35 61; Underground: Green Park*

The Verandah (101/E4)
Nice people, helpful service and good medium-priced Indian/Nepalese cooking. *Category 2; 76 Wilton Road; Tel: 0171-630 99 51; Underground: Victoria Station*

Wagamama (104/B5)
New Japanese cooking prepared in fast-food style. Noodles with all kinds of conceivable accompaniments. Ramen (hotchpotch soup). Frequented by mostly younger people wanting to eat well, substantially, quickly and cheaply. The restaurant is often very full. Tables cannot be reserved. *Category 3; 4 Streatham Street; Tel: 0171-323 92 23; Underground: Holborn*

VEGETARIAN RESTAURANTS

Mildred's (103/F5)
Popular rendezvous in Soho. Especially good salads and desserts. *Category 3; 58 Greek Street; Tel: 0171-494 16 34; Underground: Piccadilly*

Rani (O)
★ Interesting vegetarian dishes for Indian food gourmets. (*Time Out*). *Category 3; daily 6 pm–10.30 pm; 7 Long Lane; Tel: 0181-349 26 36; Underground: Finchley Central*

WINE BARS – BRASSERIES

The Archduke (112/B1)
✪ Wine bar opposite the South Bank Complex. It sometimes rattles under the railway bridge, but that does not disturb the relaxed atmosphere here. Background jazz music. The food is substantial, friendly clientele. You can often meet musicians here after a concert. *Category 3; 153 Concert Hall Approach; Tel: 0171-928 93 70; Underground: Waterloo*

The Atlantic Bar and Grill (103/E6)
Vast new restaurant-bar, the best cocktails in town. Popular with trendies. *Category 1; Mon–Sat 12 pm–2 am; 20 Glasshouse Street; Tel: 0171-734 48 88; Underground: Piccadilly Circus*

Bentley's (103/E6)
The bar is decorated with lots of marble, but despite this it is a lot

cosier than the fish restaurant above. Elegant but informal. Fish dishes such as fish pie and *clam bisque* (mussel soup) are recommended here. *Category 2; 11 Swallow Street; Tel: 0171-734 47 56; Underground: Piccadilly Circus*

The Bleeding Heart (104/C4)

Little Dorrit, a novel written by Dickens in 1855, was set here. The style of this wine bar is Victorian. British cuisine, good selection of champagne. *Category 2; Bleeding Heart Yard, Greville Street; Tel: 0171-242 82 38; Underground: Chancery Lane*

La Brasserie (110/A3)

❀ First French brasserie, beautiful Art Deco interior. The wine is expensive. Booking in advance is advisable for the evening. *Category 3; 272 Brompton Road; Tel: 0171-584 16 68; Underground: South Kensington*

Cheers (103/F6)

The bar for fans of the soap opera with the same name. *72 Regent Street; Tel: 0171-494 33 22; Underground: Piccadilly Circus*

Café Delancey (O)

★ ❀ Very popular brasserie. Tasty, reasonably priced meals. This café is a favourite meeting-place of the Camden intelligentsia. Booking in advance is advised for the evening! *Category 3; 2 Delancey Street; Tel: 0171-387 19 85; Underground: Camden Town*

Good food is also available in wine bars, brasseries and pubs

Sloane Rangers

Young people of private means and an audible *upper-class* accent. This set consists of mainly well established, wealthy individuals of sometimes aristocratic background, although some say their behaviour might not always support this. Their champagne consumption is absolutely phenomenal! They often live in the Sloane Square area and go to the country at the weekend, *of course.*

Dover Street Wine Bar (101/E1)

Jazz bar with restaurant in the basement of an old warehouse. Five minutes from Piccadilly. Music from 10 pm. *Category 2; 8–9 Dover Street West; Tel: 0171-629 98 13; Underground: Green Park*

The Hard Rock Café (110/D2)

A place of pilgrimage for all fans of the '60s. The queue in front of this well established chain of restaurant is rarely shorter than twenty people; the café is particularly popular at lunch time on Sundays. Lots of rock memorabilia as well as the famous hamburgers. Be sure to purchase a *Hard Rock* T shirt or sweater on your way out. *Category 3; 150 Old Park Lane, corner of Piccadilly; Tel: 0171-629 03 82; Underground: Hyde Park Corner*

Joe's Café (110/A5)

This is the rendezvous of London's smart set. Here champagne and even more extravagant drinks are served at the bar – as well as good coffee. Truffle cake, warm duck salad, everything is incredibly expensive, especially if you have a sit-down meal. *Category 2; 126 Draycott Avenue; Tel: 0171-225 22 17; Underground: South Kensington*

The Living Room (103/F6)

A new designer bar, where one can lounge in comfortable arm chairs and read the current newspapers, first-class cappuccino – an image of the new, relaxed Soho, where communication is regaining importance. *Category 3; 3 Bateman Street; Tel: 0171-437 48 27; Underground: Leicester Square*

Oriel (110/B5)

Directly adjacent to the famous Royal Court Theatre, not far from the King's Road. French bistro cuisine, tasty snacks. In the evening the restaurant is full of trendy socialites and *sloane rangers*. *Category 2; 50–55 Sloane Square; Tel: 0171-730 28 04; Underground: Sloane Square*

Pimlico Wine Vaults (101/E5)

Romantic vaults, good food, large selection of wines. *Category 3; Upper Tachbrook Street; Tel: 0171-834 74 29; Underground: Victoria/Pimlico*

The Rainforest Café (103/E6)

For friends of the jungle: hamburgers in a simulated tropical rainforest. *20 Shaftesbury Avenue; Tel: 0171-434 31 11; Underground: Piccadilly Circus*

Shopping with style

*London offers the finest wares for connoisseurs,
the latest fashions, cashmere from Scotland, antiques and
delicacies*

London is one of the world's greatest shopping cities. Ornately decorated and sparkling jewellery shops or ultra-chic displays are, however, rarely to be seen – you have to know where to find the best articles. London can also be very expensive, but there are lots of special offers available in the end-of-season sales at the beginning of January and July. Special end-of-line or designer sale shops offer fashions from the previous collection and second-hand shops are very popular. There are also numerous street markets. The majority of the shops in central London are open until 5.30 pm Mondays to Saturdays, some even until 8 pm. Most of the large stores stay open late one evening in the week, on different days for different shopping areas: late-closing in the West End and Kensington High Street is on Thursdays, in Knightsbridge and Chelsea it is on Wednesdays. Payment is made in cash or by credit card.

International designer fashion is mainly to be found in the following streets: ★ Sloane Street, Beauchamp Place, Bond Street, South Molton Street and ★ St Christopher's Place, ♜ Kensington High Street/Kensington Church Street (fashions for the young), Savile Row for traditional made-to-measure men's fashions, Jermyn Street for tailor-made shirts. Modern British designer clothes are available at *Browns* in South Molton Street, *Harvey Nichols* and *Harrods* as well as in the boutiques in King's Road. Precious jewellery in traditional designs is sold by the crown jewellers *Garrards* or *Mappin & Webb* – both are located in Regent Street. Bond Street has fine antique jewellery; Hatton Gardens is the centre of London's diamond trade.

Those shops that supply the Royal Family with goods can be identified by a little sign above the door with the royal coat of arms and the inscription 'By Appointment'. All very discreet, understated, elegant.

ANTIQUES

Alfies Antique Market (101/F3)
The largest antique market in London, 370 dealers under

Antiques and bric-a-brac at the flea market in Portobello Road

one roof. From antique dolls to elegant leather suitcases. *13–25 Church Street; Underground: Edgeware Road*

Camden Passage (105/D1)

★ Everything imaginable: jewellery, carpets, objets d'art, especially pieces from the 19th century. There are more antique shops in the vicinity. *Wed, Sat 8.30 am–3 pm; Upper Street; Underground: Angel*

Chelsea Antique Market (110/B5)

The cheapest of the Chelsea markets: books, prints, clothes. *245–253 King's Road; Underground: Sloane Square*

Gray's Antique Market (102/C6)

★ 200 stalls. Excellent quality, but expensive. *Mon–Fri 10 am–6 pm, closed Sat and Sun; 58 Davies Street; Underground: Bond Street*

King's Road/ Fulham Road (109/E6–F5) and (O)

There are lots of good little shops in this area which sell antique mirrors, silver, porcelain. Take time to browse. *Underground: Putney Bridge/Parsons Green*

Silver Vaults (104/C4)

★ 50 dealers display wonderful old silver in this deep vault. Some pieces are even affordable. *Mon–Fri 9 am–5.30 pm, Sat 9 am–12.30 pm; 53 Chancery Lane; Underground: Chancery Lane*

ART GALLERIES

Most of the important retail galleries for the works of old masters and modern artists are to be found in the area around the Duke of York Street and King Street as well as in Bond Street

MARCO POLO SELECTION: SHOPPING

1 Brixton Market
The Caribbean in London
(page 63)

2 Camden Passage
Victorian antiques (page 58)

3 Sloane Street
Elegant boutiques, international designer fashion
(page 57)

4 Fortnum & Mason
Salesmen in morning coats, wonderful delicatessen department (page 60)

5 Gray's Antique Market
The customers here are as noble as the goods for sale (page 58)

6 Liberty's
Very beautiful central hall, lovely materials
(page 60)

7 Leadenhall Market
Shopping in medieval surroundings (page 63)

8 Portobello Market
The best flea market
(page 62)

9 St Christopher's Place
Young fashions in a picturesque street (page 57)

10 Silver Vaults
Silver 'underground', but in absolutely perfect condition (page 58)

and Cork Street. There are also some in south-west London in the King's Road and Fulham Road. Galleries for contemporary art are located in the Portobello Road area.

AUCTION ROOMS

Viewing times are published before all auctions.

Bonham's (110/B2)
Montpelier Street; Underground: Knightsbridge

Christie's (101/F1)
8 King Street; Underground: Piccadilly Circus, Green Park

Philipp's (102/C6)
7 Blenheim Street, New Bond Street; Underground: Bond Street

Sotheby's (102/C6)
34/35 New Bond Street; Underground: Bond Street

BOOKS

The Collector magazine lists 300 dealers according to their area of specialization *(Tel: 0181-740 70 20).*

Bell, Book & Radmall (102/B6)
In a little street full of wonderful bookshops! *4 Cecil Court; Underground: Leicester Square*

Books of Charing Cross (102/B6)
Antiquarian book store. *56 Charing Cross Road; Underground: Leicester Square*

Daunt's (102/C4)
A heavenly collection of travel books. *83 Marylebone High Street; Underground: Bond Street*

Charing Cross – the 'book street'

Foyles (103/F5)
The largest and best-known bookshop in London. For those with lots of time to browse. *119–125 Charing Cross Road; Underground: Leicester Square*

CHOCOLATE AND SWEETS

Charbonell et Walker (101/E1)
Home-made chocolate truffles, exclusivly wrapped up in satin and silk. *1 The Royal Arcade, 28 Old Bond Street; Underground: Green Park*

Roccoco Chocolates (110/B5)
Handmade luxury chocolates, beautifully wrapped. *321 King's Road; Underground: Sloane Square*

COURT SUPPLIERS

Asprey's (103/D5)
Beautiful silver and precious jewellery. The aristocrats' gift shop. *165–169 New Bond Street; Underground: Bond Street*

Floris (111/E1)

Perfumers 'by royal warrant' since 1820. *89 Jermyn Street; Underground: Piccadilly Circus*

Fortnum & Mason (111/E1)

★ Aristocratic shop famous for its food department. Choice delicacies wrapped up in the store's own noble packaging. Included in the service provided are salesmen who carry the shopping baskets. Good restaurants. Designer fashion. *181 Piccadilly; Underground: Piccadilly Circus*

J. Locks & Co. (111/E2)

The London Hatters — customers are treated like royalty here. *6 St James's Street; Underground: Green Park*

Lobbs (111/E2)

The most comfortable shoes around £500 a pair. *9 St James's Street; Underground: Green Park*

Paxton & Whitfield (111/E1)

Excellent cheeses and delicacies even for those with not so much money to spend. *93 Jermyn Street; Underground: Piccadilly Circus*

Penhaligon's (104/A5)

A Mr Penhaligon was barber at the court of Queen Victoria. Wonderful scent bottles, perfumes made to original formulas. 'Bluebell' is the most famous. *41 Wellington Street; Underground: Covent Garden*

Simpsons (111/E1)

The very best kind of department store. Outfitters to the Royal Family. Top quality (own brand 'Daks'). Cashmere, international fashion. There is a sushi bar in the basement. *203 Piccadilly; Underground: Piccadilly Circus*

Twinings (104/B6)

Tea suppliers famous for their Earl Grey tea. *216 The Strand; Underground: Charing Cross*

DEPARTMENT STORES

Harvey Nichols (110/B2)

Opened in 1817. A 'supermarkt' for designer clothes on three floors. There is a good restaurant on the fifth floor. *109 Knightsbridge; Underground: Knightsbridge*

Harrods (110/B2)

Beyond all doubt *the* department store in London, but its size can also make it quite bewildering. 330 departments on a sales area of 62,705 square metres (675,000 square feet) invite you to spend your money. Their motto is: 'All things for all men everywhere'. They really do sell *everything* here, down to the famous elephant which was a present for Ronald Reagan. The 'Food Halls', decorated throughout in Art Deco tiles, are particularly worth seeing. Beautiful antiques are displayed for sale on the third floor. *87-135 Brompton Road; Underground: Knightsbridge*

Liberty's (103/E5)

★ Beautiful old department store with half-timbering made out of the planks of old men-of-war. Famous for its Liberty print silks and Varuna wools. Classical designs, some of them modelled on designs by William Morris: e.g. peacock, peony, pheasant. The squares, large headscarves, show that you have money as well as good taste. They are reasonably priced in the sales. Good young designer department, witty and practical ideas for presents.Unusual oriental articles in the basement. *200 Regent Street; Underground: Oxford Circus*

Whiteleys (O)

This new luxury shopping centre contains 80 shops: international fashion, gift shops, cafés, restaurants. There are eight cinemas on the second floor which are open until 10 pm. *Mon–Sat*

10 am–8 pm; Queensway; Underground: Bayswater

FASHION

London has been famous for its pop fashion since the '60s. But classical men's and ladie's wear still remains popular. Burberrys or Aquascutum coats or suits from Savile Row are world famous. The latest fashions can be found in the chain stores Joseph or Warehouse.

All things for all men everywhere: Harrods, the largest department store in Europe

Designs (O)
Valentino, Armani etc, and unfortunately they are still expensive even second-hand. *60 Rosslyn Hill; Underground: Hampstead*

Pandora Dress Agency (110/A3)
The largest second-hand shop of its kind: YSL, Edelstein, Oldfield for a third of the original price. 5,000 articles. *16–22 Cheval Place, behind Bonham's, Montpelier Square; Underground: Knightsbridge*

Vent (100/C5)
Interesting clothes in a new shopping district in the Ledbury Road area. *178 a Westbourne Grove; Underground: Ladbroke Grove*

Virginia's (108/A1)
Where the super models buy something special to wear (from the '40s). *98 Portland Road; Underground: Holland Park*

FLEA MARKETS

London is renowned for its markets, each with its own character and with its own bargains.

Bermondsey Market (114/A2)
Also known as the New Caledonian Market. The largest antique flea market apart from Portobello Road. Come early for the best bargains, run principally by dealers for dealers. *Friday from 7 am; Bermondsey Square; Underground: Tower Hill; bus: 78 or 42*

Camden Lock (O)
Not to be confused with Camden Passage! One of the best flea markets. Crafts, bric-a-brac, clothes and antiques. Especially interesting at weekends. *Mon–Fri 10 am–6 pm, Sat, Sun 9am–5 pm; Camden High Street; Underground: Camden Town*

Portobello Market (100/A5)
★ Still the largest and best known. Come early! Relax in the Market Bar – very trendy! *Sat 8 am–4 pm; Portobello Road; Underground: Notting Hill Gate/Ladbroke Grove*

GIFTS

As well as the shops nearly all the London museums sell pretty and useful articles.

Jo Malone (109/F5)
Perfumery for trendies and individualists who like unusual scents. *154 Walton Street; Underground: South Kensington*

Neal St East (104/A5)
A bazaar in Covent Garden, oriental and Chinese articles. *5 Neal Street; Underground: Covent Garden*

Royal Academy (101/E1)
Good art books, cards and prints. *Burlington House, Piccadilly; Underground: Piccadilly Circus*

The Singing Tree (O)
Large selection of antique miniature doll's houses for the serious collector. *69 New King's Road; Underground: Fulham Broadway*

Smythsons of Bond Street (103/D5)
The very best in note paper – high-class and expensive! *44 New Bond Street; Underground: Bond Street*

Wilde One's (110/B5)
New Age shop that sells almost everything from Red Indian moccasins to crystal goods. *383 King's Road; Underground: Sloane Square*

LINGERIE AND CHIC DESSOUS

Agent Provocateur (101/F6)
Exorbitant, but quite an experience! *6 Broadwick Street; Underground: Leicester Square*

Rigby & Peller (110/B2)
Customers are still measured and advised here – not just for luxury articles. *2 Hans Road; Underground: Knightsbridge*

Satin & Lace (O)
12 Regency Parade; Underground: Swiss Cottage

RECORDS

Tower Records (103/F6)
The super store for classic, jazz and rock. *1 Piccadilly Circus; Underground: Piccadilly Circus*

Virgin Mega Store (103/F5)
Pop. Huge CD department. Videos. *14–30 Oxford Street; Underground: Tottenham Court Road*

STREET MARKETS

There are numerous street markets in London where fruit and vegetables as well as flowers are sold. The 'Street Market' leaflet published by the London Tourist Board includes a selection of these. Particularly interesting are:

Berwick Street Market (103/E5)
Fruit and vegetable market behind Oxford Street. *Mon–Sat 9 am–5 pm; Berwick Street; Underground: Oxford Circus*

Brixton Market (O)
★ The best market in south London, full of exotic articles. Wide range of Afro-Caribbean food, fashion and music. *Mon, Tues, Thurs, Fri, Sat 9 am–5.30 pm, Wed 9 am–1 pm, closed on Sun; Electric Avenue; Underground: Brixton*

Camden Lock Market (O)
Antiques, bric-a-brac, period and Asian clothes, craft and food stalls – in idyllic surroundings, a weekend paradise. *Sat, Sun 9 am–5 pm; Camden High Street; Underground: Camden Town*

Leadenhall Market (106/A5)
★ Fish, meat and delicatessens in medieval surroundings. Picturesque cast-iron market hall dating from 1881. *Mon–Fri 7 am–3 pm; Whittington Avenue near Grace Church St.; Underground: Bank*

Portobello Market (100/A5)
Famous flea market with clothes, silver, porcelain – it is also worth exploring the neighbourhood, with its galleries and chic restaurants. *Sat from 6 am; Portobello Road; Underground: Nottinghill Gate*

Leadenhall Market during the week: fresh fish from all over the world

Sweet dreams

Where to find accommodation that is wonderfully comfortable but not terribly expensive

Finding a good but inexpensive hotel in London is not easy. Apart from the few 'secret tips' available from insiders, a good alternative which can be recommended is bed & breakfast – i.e. private accommodation. However, the price and quality of this type of accommodation can vary considerably. For better quality B&B the 'Bulldog Club' is recommended: rooms with private shower or bathroom in elegant private homes. These are certainly somewhat more expensive (£45–£75 per person), but you can rely on them being more comfortable. Club membership (£25) is required. The Bulldog Club can be contacted at *Tel: 0171-341 94 95; Fax: 341 94 96.* A useful number for finding bed & breakfast in West London is the Central London Accommodations, *Tel: 0171-602 96 68; Fax: 602 56 09,* an accommodation agency for B&B in family homes. B&B in 'homes of distinction' costs from £18 per night. The 'London B&B Agency' has rooms in north London for

around £20. *Tel: 0171-586 27 68; Fax: 586 65 67.* Uptown Reservations has rooms in Knightsbridge/Chelsea, 40 good addresses cost around £65. *Tel: 0171-351 34 45; Fax: 351 93 83.* The London Tourist Board has two large information centres at Heathrow Airport and Victoria Station, which operate booking services for all types of accommodation.

Prices for hotel accommodation usually include VAT but often do not include breakfast. You may also have to pay extra for a full English breakfast of bacon and eggs etc.

Various terms and symbols are used in Britain to classify hotels according to the different standards and rates they offer. This tends to be rather confusing. In this guide the hotels have been grouped into three different price categories. In each case the price quoted is for a double room. Lower-priced hotels (category 3) cost between £60 and £110 per night. Medium-priced hotels (category 2) cost between £100 and £165. For those guests who would like a little more luxury (category 1) a room can cost approximately £170 to £200 and more. At the end of this chapter we have also

As discreet as it is exclusive – the Connaught is one of the noblest luxury hotels in London

MARCO POLO SELECTION: HOTELS

1 The Abbey Court Hotel
Full of charm, quiet but still central (page 67)

2 The Aster House
Economical and comfortable (page 70)

3 Basil Street Hotel
Individual style, old-fashioned but not at all pompous (page 66)

4 Blakes Hotel
Very stylish, one of the exotic hotels in London (page 66)

5 11 Cadogan Square
Elegant, ideal for businessmen (page 67)

6 Hazlitts Hotel
Old-English atmosphere in the centre of Soho (pages 67–68)

7 Conrad Hotel
Harbour atmosphere in the middle of Chelsea (page 69)

8 Pembridge Court Hotel
Comfortable rooms, near Portobello Road (page 68)

9 The Portobello Hotel
Friendly hotel with a large garden (page 68)

10 Langorf Hotel
Quiet location; completely refurbished (page 70)

included a list of cheaper accommodation for young people and students.

HOTELS CATEGORY 1

(High-quality hotels for between £170 and £200)

Basil Street Hotel   (110/B3)
★ Two minutes from Harrods. Private, traditional 'country house' hotel, lots of antiques. 92 rooms. £199. *8 Basil Street; Tel: 0171-581 33 11; Fax: 581 36 93; Underground: Knightsbridge*

Beaufort Hotel   (110/B3)
Located within 70 metres (77 yds) from Harrods in a square with garden. Elegant and comfortable, each room with its own distinctive style. You can have your breakfast served in your room on Wedgewood china. It is also possible to become a member of the hotel's own fitness centre — but then an overnight stay can cost £188 and more. Five floors, lift. 28 rooms (7 suites). *33 Beaufort Gardens; Tel: 0171-584 52 52; Fax: 589 28 34; Underground: Knightsbridge*

Blakes Hotel   (109/D5)
★ An exotic hotel! Every room is individually decorated: in classic white, burgundy red and glistening emerald green velvet. The owner has fulfilled her dream of a luxury hotel here. The restaurant is very expensive. 52 rooms. £175. *33 Roland Gardens; Tel: 0171-370 67 01; Fax: 373 04 42; Underground: Gloucester Road*

Chesterfield Hotel   (102/B5)
Here you can see just how elegant the district of Mayfair can

be. 110 rooms – book yours in the old-fashioned part of the hotel, Dartmouth House. 18th-century elegance. Helpful and courteous hotel staff. £ 199. *35 Charles Street; Tel: 0171-491 26 22; Fax: 491 47 93; Underground: Bond Street*

11 Cadogan Square   (110/B4)

★ Finest residential area in Belgravia. Elegant and exclusive, suitable for businessmen. With garden. 60 rooms, the best ones are at the rear of the hotel. £ 200. *11 Cadogan Square; Tel: 0171-730 34 26; Fax: 730 52 17; Underground: Sloane Square*

HOTELS CATEGORY 2

(Medium-priced hotels between £ 100 and £ 165)

The Abbey Court Hotel   (100/C6)

★ Luxurious and functional, in country house style. Situated in a quiet street near Portobello Road. 22 rooms on three floors, no lift, but excellent service. £ 130. *20 Pembridge Gardens; Tel: 0171-221 75 18; Fax: 792 08 58; Underground: Notting Hill*

Academy Hotel   (103/F4)

Friendly, clean hotel with patio, in the centre of London. 50 rooms, no lift. £ 120. *17–21 Gower Street; Tel: 0171-631 41 15; Fax: 636 34 42; Underground: Goodge Street*

Berner's Park Plaza   (103/E5)

Situated in a quiet side street off Oxford Street. Beautiful lounge where harp music is played in the afternoons. 237 comfortable and practical rooms. Generous breakfast buffet. £ 150. Suitable for disabled visitors. *10 Berner Street; Tel: 0171-636 16 29; Fax: 580 39 72; Underground: Tottenham Court Road*

Cavendish Forte
Crest St Jame's James'   (101/E1)

This hotel is as noble as its surroundings in old-fashioned and elegant Jermyn Street, directly behind Piccadilly. Modern furnishings, with a popular gentlemen's club style bar. 256 rooms. £ 150. *81 Jermyn Street; Tel: 0171-930 21 11; Fax: 839 21 25; Underground: Piccadilly Circus/ Green Park*

Durrants Hotel   (103/D6)

Ninety-six rooms, all in nostalgic English style. Very central, close to Bond Street and Oxford Street shopping areas. £ 115. *George Street; Tel: 0171-935 81 31; Fax: 487 35 10; Underground: Bond Street or Oxford Circus*

The Gore Hotel   (109/E4)

Near Hyde Park, popular with people in the media and music branches. Modernized hotel furnished in Victorian style. 54 rooms; lift. £ 150. *189 Queen's Gate; Tel: 0171-584 66 01; Fax: 589 81 27; Underground: Gloucester Road*

Hazlitts Hotel   (103/E5)

★In the middle of Soho – two minutes from Ronnie Scott's Jazz Club. A rarity: an old house which has preserved its original style. Approx. 2,000 pictures; old-English atmosphere. The hotel has been completely modernized. 23 rooms. Those to the rear of the building are quiet, the basement apartment has a small garden. No lift. £ 148. *6 Frith*

It is not difficult to live in comfort and luxury in London – but this of course has its price!

Street; Tel: 0171-434 17 71; Fax: 439 15 24; Underground: Leicester Square

L'Hotel (110/B3)
Very small hotel with private house atmosphere (directly next to the elegant Capitol). Very helpful staff. In the basement there is a good wine bar, *Le Métro,* where food is also served. 100 m (330 ft) from Harrods. 12 rooms. £ 146 incl. breakfast. *28 Basil Street; Tel: 0171-589 62 86; Fax: 225 00 11; Underground: Knightsbridge*

Jury's Kensington (109/E4)
Recently refurbished, includes an Irish bar and a nightclub. 182 rooms. £ 145. *109 Queensgate; Tel: 0171-589 63 00; Fax: 581 14 92; Underground: South Kensington*

Knightsbridge Green Hotel (110/B3)
Ideally situated for shopping in Knightsbridge. Pleasant accommodation in 16 apartments and 4 double rooms. No restaurant. Conveniently organized: the room key also unlocks the front door. Lift. £ 125. *159 Knightsbridge; Tel: 0171-584 62 74; Fax:*

225 16 35; Underground: Knightsbridge

Pembridge Court Hotel (100/C6)
★ 'Town house' style, 26 comfortable rooms. £ 165 incl. English breakfast plus VAT. *34 Pembridge Gardens; Tel: 0171-229 99 77; Fax: 727 49 82; Underground: Notting Hill Gate*

The Portobello Hotel (100/B6)
★ This small hotel is part of a row of smart Victorian terrace houses. Picturesque area. There is a large garden behind the hotel. Portobello Road is just round the corner. 30 pretty rooms. Friendly owners. Lift. £ 140. *22 Stanley Gardens; Tel: 0171-727 27 77; Fax: 792 96 41; Underground: Notting Hill Gate*

Regency Hotel (109/E4)
Near the Victoria & Albert Museum. 210 rooms, fitness centre. Large old but completely refurbished Regency house. Conference facilities. Centrally located, yet quiet in the evenings. £ 135. *100–106 Queen's Gate; Tel: 0171-370 45 95; Fax: 370 55 55; Underground: South Kensington*

The Hotel Russell (104/A4)
Situated in Bloomsbury, overlooking the gardens of a large square. Elegant buffet restaurant, stylish bar. 328 rooms. £ 155. *Russell Square; Tel: 0171-837 64 70; Fax: 837 28 57; Underground: Russell Square*

Searcy's (110/B2)
Small hotel with 11 elegant old-fashioned rooms and a private garden. Located in Knightsbridge round the corner from Harrods. £ 112 incl. breakfast. *30*

Luxury hotels in London

Conrad Hotel (O)

Modern comfort in the waterfront area of Chelsea. Suites from £ 220, penthouses from £ 1,400 (negotiable). Buffet brunch on Sundays for £ 35 (incl. ½ bottle of champagne). Book a table at the window! Business Centre for businessmen, fitness club. Facilities for the disabled. 160 rooms. *Chelsea Harbour; Tel: 0171-823 30 00; Fax: 351 65 25; Underground: Sloane Square*

The Connaught (102/C6)

As discreet as it is exclusive. Impressive oak stairway, antique furniture, flowers everywhere – old English luxury. 90 rooms. From £ 360. *Carlos Place; Tel:0171-499 70 70; Fax: 495 32 62; Underground: Bond Street*

The Dorchester (110/C2)

For the past six years it has belonged to the Sultan of Brunei, who paid 72 million pounds to have it refurbished in new splendour but in its original style. The *Oriental* restaurant has a Michelin star and is worth visiting. Wonderful view from here over Hyde Park. 252 rooms (50 suites). From £ 317 for a single room to £ 1,468 for suites. Facilities for the disabled. *53 Park Lane; Tel and Fax: 0171-629 88 88; Underground: Hyde Park Corner*

Halcyon Hotel (108/A1)

In central, quiet location. From outside it looks like an enormous private house, but inside is pure luxury. Very discreet, therefore popular with stars and celebrities. 44 rooms. From £ 250. *81 Holland Park; Tel: 0171-727 72 88; Fax: 229 85 16; Underground: Holland Park*

The Lanesborough (110/C2)

Classical luxury combined with modern business life: butler and fax machines. A big hit: an outing to *Manoir aux Quatres Saisons* near Oxford in the champagne bus. In the summer for lunch, about £ 100 – expensive, but idyllic! To book, ring *Tel: 01844-27 88 81.* 95 rooms. From £ 287 to £ 3,500 for a suite! Facilities for the disabled. *Hyde Park Corner; Tel: 0171-259 55 99; Fax: 259 56 06; Underground: Hyde Park Corner*

Le Meridien Picadilly (101/E1)

This is one of the most elegant old hotels since it was refurbished at a cost of £16 million. Fantastic decor in the restaurants, piano and harp music, crystal chandeliers and vast bouquets of flowers, first-class cuisine. The rooms are well furnished, but rather small; however, there is an excellent 'Health Club' with a good swimming pool which is free to guests. 263 rooms. £ 323. *Piccadilly, Tel and Fax: 0171-734 80 00; Underground: Piccadilly*

The Landmark (102/B3)

This former station is now decorated in oriental style and even includes an atrium shaded by palm trees (45 m/150 ft high!). 309 rooms. From £ 264. Facilities for the disabled. *222 Marylebone Road; Tel: 0171-631 80 00; Fax: 631 80 33; Underground: Marylebone*

Pavilion Road; Tel: 0171-584 49 21; Fax: 823 86 94; Underground: South Kensington

16 Sumner Place (110/A4)

Five minutes from Brompton Road; very close to Chelsea. Quiet, small hotel, 36 rooms. Comfortable public rooms, small single rooms. Mini conservatory and lift. £ 150 incl. breakfast. *16 Sumner Place; Tel: 0171-589 52 32; Fax: 584 86 15; Underground: South Kensington*

HOTELS CATEGORY 3

(Lower-priced hotels between £ 60 and £ 110)

The Alfa Hotel (O)

42 comfortable rooms, the best of which are on the first floor. £ 63. *78 Warwick Way; Tel: 0171-828 86 03; Fax: 976 65 36; Underground: Victoria*

The Aster House (110/A4)

★ 12 pleasant, well-furnished rooms, breakfast is served in the conservatory. £ 85, four-poster bed £ 115. *3 Summer Place; Tel:0171-581 58 88; Fax:584 49 25; Underground: South Kensington*

Bryanston Court Hotel (102/B5)

Situated in a quiet street at the end of Oxford Street near Marble Arch. 56 small, practical rooms. Pleasant staff. £ 90 incl. breakfast. *56–60 Great Cumberland Place; Tel: 0171-262 31 41; Fax: 262 72 48; Underground: Marble Arch*

The Colonnade Hotel (103/D3)

Situated in the picturesque district of 'Little Venice'. Friendly owners, good value for money! 50 rooms. £ 110 incl. English breakfast. *2 Warrington Crescent; Tel: 0171-286 10 52; Fax: 286 10 57; Underground: Warwick Avenue*

Langorf Hotel (O)

★ For £ 90 incl. breakfast you can live in a completely refurbished house in the lovely Hampstead area. A medium-rate hotel with a high standard of comfort (good showers!). Furnishings functional yet elegant. 32 rooms. £ 82. *20 Frognal; Tel: 0171-794 44 83; Fax: 435 90 55; Underground: Finchley Road*

Lincoln House Hotel (102/B5)

In a very central location not far from the many attractions of Hyde Park. This hotel is comfortable and reasonably priced. 20 rooms £ 79. *33 Gloucester Place; Tel: 0171-935 70 89; Fax: 486 01 66; Underground: Marble Arch*

In the Marco Polo Spirit

Marco Polo was the first true world traveller. He travelled with peaceful intentions forging links between the East and the West. His aim was to discover the world, and explore different cultures and environments without changing or disrupting them. He is an excellent role model for the 20th-century traveller. Wherever we travel we should show respect for other cultures and natural environments.

WWF

La Reserve (O)

Elegant, yet reasonably priced. 43 small, practical rooms. £85. Marco Polo readers are given a double room if they book a single room here (at no extra charge). *422 Fulham Road; Tel: 0171-385 85 61; Fax: 385 76 62; Underground: Fulham Broadway*

Winchester Hotel (110/C3)

Eighteen small but well-furnished, comfortable rooms. Five minutes from Victoria Station. £65 incl. breakfast. *17 Belgrave Road; Tel: 0171-828 29 72; Underground: Victoria*

Windermere Hotel (101/E5)

This hotel is situated only 10 minutes from Victoria Station. Pleasant and comfortable rooms with courteous service. Evening meals. £78. 23 rooms. *142–144 Warwick Way; Tel: 0171-834 51 63; Underground: Victoria*

CHILDREN

Most hotels try to be accommodating to children by allowing them to sleep in their parents' room, for which there is usually an extra charge. However, because of the size of some of the rooms that are available, this is not always possible and discretion is asked for in a situation of this sort.

HOME FROM HOME

Apartments are often a more economical and spacious alternative for families. The British Travel Centre at Victoria Station has a list of this form of accomodation. However, flats are often not as comfortable as expected.

Please send a written request detailing your wishes and book as far in advance as possible. It is advisable to negotiate through a reputable agent

YOUTH HOSTELS

There are several youth hostels in London. Youth hostel accommodation is available to holders of a valid youth hostel membership card. Book as far ahead as possible with the YHA *(Youth Hostels Association). (National Office of YHA: 01727-85 52 15).* Cheap accommodation is also available in YMCA hotels *(National Council number: 0181-520 55 99, or ask at the YMCA office in London, Tel: 0171-723 00 71; Fax: 0172-784 61 70).* Very nice: Holland House YHA, *Tel: 0171-937 07 48; Fax: 376 06 67.* Carter Lane Youth Hostel, *Tel: 0171-236 49 65, near St Paul's Cathedral*

Ideal in the summer holidays: university and college accommodation, e.g. LSE High Holborn, *Tel: 0171-379 55 89; Fax: 379 56 40.* Good quality and inexpensive: rooms which sleep four for £50 from the Travel Inn chain of hotels; *Tel: 0158-241 43 41.*

It is possible to book hotels near London for groups, also through the YHA *(Tel: see above or 0171-730 57 69)* or through the IBN *(International Booking Network) in USA (Washington); Tel: (202) 783 6161 or Canada (Montreal); Tel: 514-2523 117.*

Norfolk Court Hotel (101/F5)

First-class breakfast, friendly staff, simple rooms from £28 single, £44 double. *20 Norfolk Square; Tel: 0171-723 49 63; Underground: Paddington*

The London calender

New Year's Eve in Trafalgar Square, Ascot in June …
The most important social and cultural events of the year

There is always something on in London – traditional, cultural or sporting events. Whether it is the magnificent Royal Tournament or Notting Hill Carnival, the Caribbean carnival, the Chelsea Antiques Fair or the Regent Street Lights, the glittering Christmas decorations so popular with children, or various New Year parades, there is always something to admire and celebrate.

PUBLIC HOLIDAYS

1 January; Good Friday; Easter Monday; Bank Holidays are the first and last Mondays in May and the last Monday in August; 25 and 26 December.

Most museums are closed on public holidays although the majority of pulic places are open. Some shops, especially the 24-hour supermarkets and gasoline/service stations do business. Only a few restaurants are open.

Members of the Household Cavalry dressed in their magnificent ceremonial uniforms

SPECIAL EVENTS

January

1 January: the London Parade in the centre of London around Piccadilly/Trafalgar Square. End of January/beginning of February: the *Chinese New Year Celebrations* in Soho. (**103/F6**)
The London Contemporary Art Fair – modern British art; *Tel: 0171-3593535*

February/March

Ash Wednesday: *Cakes and Ale Sermon* church service for members of the Stationers' Company in their traditional costumes, when cakes and ale are distributed. (**105/E5**) *Crypt of St Paul's Cathedral*; *Underground: Mansion House*

March

13–24 March: *Chelsea Antiques Fair*, including some antiques from before 1830. Amazing selection, but expensive. (**110/B5**) *Underground: Sloane Square*

March/April

Maundy Thursday: *Royal Maundy* in Westminster Abbey. Distribution of money by the Queen to the poor. (**112/A3**) *Underground: Westminster*

Easter Monday: The *London Harness Horse Parade* in Battersea Park. Colourful parade, funfair. (**O**) *British Rail: Battersea Park Station*

Date varies: *ADT World Marathon.* The largest marathon in the world – with 175,000 participants. *Info: Tel: 0171-948 79 35*

23 April: Shakespeare's death is commemorated with *readings* in Southwark Cathedral. (**113/F1**) *Info: Tel: 0171-407 37 08; Underground: London Bridge*

May

Covent Garden Festival (**104/B5**) *Info: Tel: 0181-944 94 67*

End of May: *Beating Retreat by the Household Division Massed Bands.* 500 musicians from the guard regiments on the parade grounds at Horse Guards Parade. Very impressive event! (**112/A1–2**) *Whitehall; Underground: Charing Cross*

June

The Modern Dance and Theatre Festival Lift, *Tel: 0171-336 05 08*

Saturday nearest 11 June: *Trooping the Colour.* Birthday parade for the Queen in Horse Guards Parade. (**112/A1–2**) *Whitehall; Underground: Charing Cross*

24 June: *Election of the Sheriffs of the City of London.* Colourful public ceremony. (**105/F5**) *Guildhall; Underground: Bank*

End of June: ★ *Royal Ascot.*

The main event of the horse-racing season. Thursday is 'Ladies' Day', when the colourful assortment of hats are of greater importance than the horses. (**O**) *Ascot Racecourse, Ascot, Berkshire; British Rail: Waterloo-Ascot, 10 min to race course*

June/July: *International Lawn Tennis Championships* at Wimbledon. (**O**) *British Rail: Wimbledon*

10 June to end of August: *Royal Academy Summer Exhibition.* (**101/E1**) Contemporary British art.

July

Last week of June/first two weeks of July: *City of London Festival, Tel: 0171-377 05 40* (**105/E–F 5**)

Mid-July: *Spitalfields Festival, Info: Tel: 0171-377 13 62*

Mid-July: for all garden-lovers: the largest *Flower Show* in the world at Hampton Court. (**O**) *British Rail: Hampton Court*

Mid–end of July: *Royal Tournament.* Impressive military spectacle. (**108/C5**) *Earl's Court Exhibition Centre; Underground: Earl's Court*

Mid-July – mid-August: *The Proms.* Classical music concerts every day in the Royal Albert Hall. (**109/E2**) *Advance booking: Tel: 0171-589 82 12*

August

Last weekend in August: ★ *Notting Hill Carnival.* Caribbean immigrants celebrate with spectacular and imaginative processions. (**100/A–B6**) *Underground: Notting Hill Gate*

October

First Sunday in October: *Costermongers' Harvest Festival.* Service attended by the Pearly Kings and Queens. (**112/A1**) *St-Martin-in-the-Fields, Trafalgar Square; Underground: Charing Cross*

November

First Sunday in November: *Veteran Car Run* from London to Brighton. Early morning start from Hyde Park Corner. (**110/C2**) *Underground: Hyde Park Corner*

5 November: *Guy Fawkes Day* (**112/A3**). Firework displays to celebrate the discovery of the plot to blow up Parliament in 1605.

Second Saturday in November: ★ *Lord Mayor's Show.* Magnificent procession of the Lord Mayor of the City of London. (**105/F5**) *Underground: Bank*

Mid-November: ★ *State Opening of Parliament.* The Queen rides from Buckingham Palace to the Houses of Parliament in a golden state coach. (**111–112/A2–E3**)

Mid-Nov–Dec (**103/C5–E6**): *Christmas Lights* in Regent Street and Oxford Street.

27 November: *Christmas Parade* in the centre of London. (**111/E6**)

December

31 December: *New Year's Eve Celebrations* at midnight in Trafalgar Square. Singing and dancing around the fountains. Can be *very* crowded. (**112/A1**) *Underground: Charing Cross*

Royal Ascot, where the hats are sometimes more important than the horses

Nightlife

*Cosy pubs, exclusive clubs, trendy discotheques,
musicals, classical and rock concerts: London has it all*

Even for the most energetic it should prove impossible to enjoy more than a fraction of the wide range of entertainment which London has to offer. There are numerous events – plays, concerts, ballet performances – every evening. Magazines such as *Time Out* and *What's On* and the *Evening Standard* (especially the *Hot Tickets* leaflet published on Thursdays) can be helpful. Tickets should be booked as far in advance as possible; it is cheapest to purchase them direct from the theatre box office or to make a telephone booking and pay by credit card. Agencies charge a booking fee (approx. 20% of the value of the ticket). Telephone numbers of ticket agencies can be found amongst the theatre listings. Beware of *ticket touts* outside theatres and concert halls who offer tickets for popular shows at exorbitant prices – and sometimes even sell forgeries!

Discotheques and pubs are just as popular with Londoners as with tourists. Pubs are a traditional part of the British way of life. Discotheques and other dance clubs vary according to the age and income of their patrons: centres of the latest avant-garde music alternate between high-tech trendy nightclubs and exclusive establishments that require you to be member.

There is good live music to be heard every evening. Nowhere else is there such a lively rock and pop scene as in London. World-famous stars give guest performances in the Royal Albert Hall and Wembley Stadium. House, rave and techno events are all listed in *Time Out*.

CINEMAS

The main cinemas are centred around Leicester Square and Haymarket. The first perfor-

The large cinemas showing first releases are located in and around Leicester Square

mance usually begins about 2 pm, the last either around 8 pm or 9.45 pm. There are late showings on Fridays and Saturdays from 11 pm. Prices range from £ 5–£ 9.

Chelsea Cinema (110/B5)
You can see the best new international films in plush surroundings here. *262 King's Road; Tel: 0171-351 37 42; Underground: Sloane Square*

Curzon Cinema (111/D2)
An exceptionally interesting cinema. International films. *Curzon Street, Mayfair; Tel: 0171-99 37 37; Underground: Green Park*

Everyman Cinema (O)
A former theatre. The oldest *repertory cinema* in the world. Programme changes daily. Wonderfully shabby. *Holly Bush Vale, Hampstead High Street; Tel: 0171-435 15 25; Underground: Hampstead (diagonally opposite)*

National Film Theatre (112/B1)
In the South Bank Arts Centre. The London Film Festival takes place here every year in autumn. *Tel: 0171-928 32 32; Underground: Embankment*

Odeon Leicester Square (103/F6)
The largest cinema in London showing first releases. 1,965 seats in one auditorium. *Leicester Square; Tel: 0171-930 61 11; Underground: Leicester Square*

Virgin Trocadero Cinema (103/F6)
A huge IMAX screen as well as seven other cinemas in the Trocadero Centre. *13 Coventry Street; Tel: 0171-970 60 15; Underground Piccadilly Circus*

CONCERTS

London has a wealth of classical music of unrivalled quality to offer. Tickets for concerts are good value and cost between about £ 7 to £ 30. The most important London orchestras are: *The Philharmonia, The Royal Philharmonic Orchestra* and *The London Philharmonic Orchestra* as well as the *London Symphony Orchestra,* which is based at the Barbican Centre. The *Academy of St Martin-in-the-Fields* give concerts in the church of the same name. The church concerts in St John's, Smith Square are often outstanding – and there is a good bistro in the crypt. On Sundays there are concerts in the Wigmore Hall.

Barbican Hall (105/E4)
The building itself is controversial, but the acoustics are fantastic. Good restaurant: *Searcey's; Tel: 0171-588 30 08; The Barbican Centre; Tel: 0171-628 87 95; Underground: Barbican*

The Forum (O)
Jazz and rock club. Well-known bands, good atmosphere. Book in advance! *9/17 Highgate Road; Tel: 0171-284 22 00; Underground: Kentish Town*

St John's Smith Square (111/F3)
Smith Square; Tel: 0171-222 10 61/ 928 30 02; Underground: Westminster

Royal Albert Hall (109/E2)
Kensington Gore; Tel: 0171-589 82 12; Underground: South Kensington

South Bank (112/B1)
★ A complex of buildings in the concrete style of the '60s, which

MARCO POLO SELECTION: ENTERTAINMENT

1 Almeida
Finest alternative
theatre (page 80)

2 The Theatre Royal
The most elegant theatre
from the turn of the century,
tasteful (page 86)

3 Everyman Cinema
Originaly a theatre, now
a Art Nouveau cinema
(page 78)

4 Dingwalls
Recommended every Thurs-
day: Club Montepulciano
(page 80)

5 George Inn
Picturesque pub with a
long-standing tradition
(page 84)

6 Limelight
Exciting discotheque for
trendies – in an
old church (page 80)

7 Ronnie Scott's Club
Still the best
jazz club in London
(pages 84–85)

8 Dickens Inn
Cosy pub at
St Katharine Dock
(page 84)

9 South Bank
Concerts and drama by the
Thames (pages 78–79)

10 Wembley Stadium
Gigantic open-air
venue for stars and shows
(page 79)

includes various concert halls, where mainly classical music is performed, and the National Theatre (NT). Concerts are held in the Queen Elizabeth Hall, the Royal Festival Hall (RFH) and the Purcell Room. *South Bank; Tel: 0171-928 31 91; Underground: Waterloo.* For eating in style high above the Thames: *The People's Palace;Tel: 0171-928 99 99,* it is cheaper in the RFH or the NT and also at the *Terrace Café; Tel: 0171-401 83 61; Underground: Waterloo*

Wembley Stadium/ Wembley Arena (O)

★ Pop concerts are held in the stadium and shows in the arena. Seating for 72,000 spectators. *Empire Way; Tel: 0181-900 12 34*

and 902 88 33; Underground: Wembley Park, 12 minutes journey from Baker Street

Wigmore Hall (102/C5)

Classical concerts on Sunday mornings. *36 Wigmore Street; Tel: 0171-935 21 41;Underground: Bond Street*

DISCOTHEQUES, CLUBS, DINNER DANCING

One-nighters (club evenings that are on only once and have a special theme) are listed in the 'Club Section' of *Time Out.* Not a lot happens before 11 pm! A special service on offer is the Party Express (party bus) to the various discotheques. *Fri, Sat; Tel: 0171-630 60 63; £20*

Dingwalls (O)

★ The Club Montepulciano can be recommended here — roulette, hairdressers, clowns. *Every 2nd Thurs 7.30 pm–1 am; Camden Lock; Underground: Camden Town*

Iceni (112/E1)

A club catering for various music tastes. Three floors. *1 White Horse Street; Tel: 0171-495 53 33; Underground: Green Park*

The Jazz Café (O)

Popular jazz club with a wide range of music. Book in advance! *5 Parkway; Tel: 0171-916 60 60; Underground: Camden Town*

Limelight (103/F6)

★ In what used to be a church this popular club features lots of one-night shows. *136 Shaftesbury Avenue; Underground: Leicester Square*

Mme Jojos (103/E6)

Transvestite bar, easy-listening club – including a Burt Bacharach revival! *Tues 9 pm–2 am; 8 Brewer Street; Underground: Piccadilly Circus*

Ministry of Sound (113/E3)

Trendy club. One-nighters for house, rap and garage music. Starts at 2 o'clock in the morning and goes on till 9 am. *103 Gaunt Street; Underground: Elephant & Castle*

100 Club (103/F5)

A famous jazz/rock club, very trendy at the moment. *100 Oxford Street; Underground: Tottenham Court Road*

The Roof Garden (108/C3)

This club is situated in a roof-top garden high above Kensington. Open to non-members on Thursdays and Saturdays. £ 38. This includes an evening meal. Be sure to book in advance! *99 Kensington High Street; Tel: 0171-937 79 94; Underground: High Street Kensington*

The Velvet Underground (103/F5)

For trendies and yuppies and young people around 20. Admission £6–10. *143 Charing Cross Road; Tel: 0171-439 46 55; Underground: Tottenham Court Road*

FRINGE AND EXPERIMENTAL THEATRES

Almeida (O)

★ ❂ Contemporary repertoire; featuring cabaret performances, theatre and music festivals. *206 Upper Street; Tel: 0171-359 44 04; Underground: Angel*

Hampstead Theatre Club (O)

❂ Innovative repertoire, many new plays move on from here to the West End. *The Swiss Cottage Centre; Tel: 0171-722 93 01; Underground: Swiss Cottage*

Riverside Studios (O)

Small-scale cultural centre. Cinema, theater, live shows. *Crisp Road; Tel: 0181-748 33 54 Underground: Hammersmith*

MUSICALS

Musicals produced in London are gaining a world-wide reputation for high-quality entertainment and are becoming so popular that it is not easy to get tickets for them, especially at weekends. There is a better chance of tickets still being ob-

The oval Royal Albert Hall seats 5,500 spectators

tainable for matinée performances. *The London Theatre* is available free of charge in all the theatres. It is best to book by phone and pay by credit card. Tickets for some shows are available from 12 noon on the day of the performance at half price from the Half Price Ticket Booth in Leicester Square – although tickets for musicals are rare. Otherwise, order your tickets in advance from Ticketmaster; *Tel: 0171-344 44 44*, First Call, *Tel: 0171-497 99 77.* Here is a list of he most popular musicals (as listed in *The London Theatre*):

Beauty and the Beast (103/E5)
Dominion Theatre, Tottenham Court Road; Tel: 0171-416 60 60, Underground: Tottenham Court Road

Buddy (104/A6)
Strand Theatre, Aldwych; Tel: 0171-930 88 00; Underground: Covent Garden/Charing Cross

Cats (104/A5)
New London, Drury Lane; Tel: 0171-405 00 72; Underground: Covent Garden/Holborn

Jesus Christ Superstar (112/A1)
Lyceum Theatre, Wellington Street; Tel: 0171-656 18 03; Underground: Charing Cross

Martin Guerre (103/F6)
Prince Edward, Old Compton Street; Tel: 0171-447 54 00; Underground: Leicester Square

Les Misérables (103/F5)
Palace, Shaftesbury Av; Tel: 0171-434 09 09; Underground: Leicester Square

Oliver (103/E5)
London Palladium, 8 Argyll Street; Tel: 0171-494 50 20; Underground: Oxford Circus

The Phantom of the Opera (111/F1)
Her Majesty's, Haymarket; Tel: 0171-494 54 00; Underground: Piccadilly Circus

Starlight Express (111/D–E4)
Apollo, Wilton Road; Tel: 0171-416 60 38; Underground: Victoria Station

The Place (103/F2)
17 Dukes Road; Tel: 0171-387 09 61; Underground: Euston

Royal Opera House (104/A–B5)
Temporarily closed for refurbishment. *Covent Garden, Bow Street; Tel: 0171-240 10 66; Underground: Covent Garden*

Sadler's Wells Theatre (104/C2–3)
Rosebery Avenue; Tel: 0171-278 89 16; Underground: Angel/Farringdon

OPERA AND BALLET

International stars can be seen at Covent Garden. Seats are expensive and hard to come by. The home of the English National Opera is the London Coliseum in St Martin's Lane. Performances are sung in English here. Returns (returned tickets) are available from 6.30 pm at reduced prices. Two ballet troupes are world-famous: the *Royal Ballet*, whose home is the Royal Opera House, and the *English National Ballet*, which is based in the London Coliseum. The *London Contemporary Dance Company* performs in The Place; the Riverside Studios play host to the *Ballet Rambert*; the *London Festival Ballet* and other contemporary dance performances can be seen at Sadler's Wells Theatre. The annual *Dance Umbrella Festival* takes place in the Riverside Studios from the middle of October to the middle of November.

London Coliseum (104/A6)
St Martin's Lane; Tel: 0171-836 31 61; Underground: Leicester Square

PUBS

The most famous British institution apart from the monarchy! They were already a feature in Roman times, when Caesar wrote about the famous *ale houses*. Even the most reserved Englishman will talk at length about his 'local' with great enthusiasm – which perhaps shows the important part played by this institution in the British way of life. The pub is not only a home from home but also a public house, with its own rules that customers must observe. These rules still include restricted opening hours. Thanks to new

This pub in Northumberland Avenue always attracts a lot of customers

laws they have become more flexible recently — theoretically every pub can now stay open from 10.30 am to 11 pm. However, in practice, every landlord decides for himself at present – thereby producing wonderful chaos for tourists. You can count on pubs being open: Mon–Sat 10.30 am to 2.30 pm and 5.30 pm–11 pm, Sun 12 pm–2 pm and 7 pm–10.30 pm. All the pubs in the City are closed in the evenings – most of them are also closed at weekends. Children *should* not be allowed in, but that regulation has become more flexible too. These rules are not as traditional as they might seem – they were first introduced during World War I because Lloyd George, the Prime Minister, was concerned about the reliability of the workers in the ammunition factories. The time allowed for a lunch time pint was therefore limited. A few tips: beer is sold in pints (= 0.57 l or 1.2 American pints) or half pints; real British beer is called ale or bitter, lager is more like American or European beer. Try draught, real beer from the barrel, such as Ruddle's, Sam Smith's or Young's. In a chain of pubs called the 'XY … and Firkin' you can buy beer that has been brewed on the premises. In *The Yorkshire Grey Brewery, 2- Theobald's Road* (**104/B4**), you can even watch this process in the cellar. Drinks are bought at the bar – only regulars are allowed to buy the barkeeper a drink; tipping is absolutely out. Drinks have to be paid for immediately.

The latest development on the pub scene is the comic cabaret. These stand up comics are enormously popular. Those who are not witty enough are booed off. As well as these there are jazz pubs, which have been in existence for a long time and are now becoming more popular again. Some of them have a remarkably high standard. Pub theatres have a long tradition in London – some of them are excellent. The old English sing along pubs are sadly disappearing – so go now! Another British phenomenon is the drag pub, where the audience is entertained with transvestite shows. The latest trend is the London Café society which meets up in bars and clubs for a chat.

There are more than 7,000 pubs in London. Here is a list of some of the most interesting establishments on offer. Have a good time discovering your own 'local'.

Angel (113/F1)

Very famous 15th-century pub built on piles. *101 Bermondsey Wall East; Tel: 0171-237 36 08; Underground: London Bridge*

Anglesea Arms (O)

Excellent modern pub and restaurant. Get there early! *35 Wingate Road; Tel: 0181-749 12 91; Underground: Ravenscourt Park (Hammersmith 10 min walk)*

Black Lion (O)

Victorian pub, not many tourists, with friendly, often Irish customers. Directly opposite the *Tricycle Theatre*. You will find that there are many more old-fashioned pubs in Kilburn High Road. *274 Kilburn High Road; Tel: 0171-472 23 51; Underground: West Hampstead*

Café Theatre Club (104/A6)

❧ Artistically ambitious performances by the Artaud Company, that features three different plays every evening. *Ecology Centre, 45 Shelton Street; Tel: 0171-240 95 82; Underground: Covent Garden*

Comedy Store (103/F6)

Best-known pub for cabaret, with a critical audience known to boo performers off the stage if they are not up to standard. Interesting – but often queues from 8 pm. Charge for admission. *Closed Mon and Tues; Leicester Square; Tel: 0171-839 66 65; Underground: Leicester Square*

Dickens Inn (O)

★ At St Katharine Dock, surrounded by old sailing ships. Real ale. *St Katharine's Way; Tel: 0171-488 22 08; Underground: Tower Hill*

George Inn (114/A1)

★ Oldest 'galleried inn' (pub with an inner gallery) in London, overlooking a central courtyard. Performances in honour of Shakespeare on 23 May. *77 Borough High Street; Tel: 0171-407 20 56; Underground: London Bridge*

The George & Vulture (105/F5)

Oldest pub restaurant in the City. *Only open at lunch time, 3 Castle Court, off St Michael's Alley; Tel: 0171-626 97 10; Underground: Bank, Cornhill exit*

Jack Straws Castle (O)

⌇ Lovely area, large terrace. *North End Way; Tel: 0171-435 88 85; Underground: Hampstead*

Jazz Café (O)

First-class jazz music. Mediterranean cuisine at very reasonable prices. *5 Parkway; Tel: 0171-284 43 58; Underground: Camden*

Julie's Wine Bar (108/A1)

Almost like a film set: late Victorian kitsch with an oriental flair. Excellent food, rather off-beat clientele. *135, Portland Road; Tel: 0171-727 79 85; Underground: Holland Park*

King's Head (104/C1)

❧ Most popular pub theatre in London. Meals available before and music after the performance. *115 Upper Street; Tel: 0171-354 34 90; Underground: Angel*

O'Hanlons (104/C1)

Real Irish pub in Finsbury – with Irish Stew from John O'Hanlon's mother and beer brewed on the premises. *8 Tysoe Street; Tel: 0171-278 72 38; Underground: Angel*

The Peasant (104/C1)

New cosy pub, popular with Londoners. *240 St. John Street; Tel: 0171-33 67 26; Underground: Angel*

Prince Alfred (101/E3)

This cosy pub has hardly changed since 1862. *5 A Formosa Street; Underground: Warwick Avenue*

The Red Lion (111/F1)

Superb engraved glass and Victorian mirrors. Very small, so usually crowded. Good lunches. *2 Duke of York Street; Tel: 0171-930 20 30; Underground: Piccadilly Circus*

Ronnie Scott's Club (103/E5)

★ Most popular jazz club in London: programme starts at 10 pm

The World of Gentlemen

'Clubland', where women are only tolerated, is centred around Pall Mall and St James's Street. The last bastions of the Victorian age: Boodles, 28 St James's Street; its neighbour Brooks; The Carlton, 69 St James's, and the Athenaeum Club, 107 Pall Mall – the 'old boy network' is still alive and flourishing in London.

and goes on till 3 o'clock in the morning! Food is good, but expensive. Atmosphere unique and well worth the entrance fee. The programme is published in the London magazines. *47 Frith Street, Soho; Tel: 0171-439 07 04; Underground: Leicester Square*

Scarsdale Arms   (108/B4)
Pleasant pub with lots of flowers. Original Victorian windows. Good food, wide range of traditional beers. There is also a pretty garden. *23 Edwardes Square; Tel: 0171-937 45 13; Underground: Kensington High Street*

The Three Tuns   (102/C5)
Behind Selfridges, ideal for a breather after shopping in Oxford Street. Original decor – enjoy it with a reasonably priced lunch. *1 Portman Mews South; Tel: 0171-408 03 30; Underground: Marble Arch*

Waxy O'Connors Irish Pub   (110/F1)
A pub for 1,000 people – and this maze of rooms is often as full as that. Friendly people, good beer and good food. *14–16 Rupert Street; Tel: 0171-287 02 55; Underground: Piccadilly*

PROSTITUTION

There is no 'official' Eros centre in London. In Soho first names on some doors make it plain what is on offer there. Shepherd Market in Mayfair also has red lights in some windows and ladies discreetly strolling about. Homosexual prostitution is to be found around Piccadilly Circus and King's Cross. Such activities are often linked with clubs here.

SWIMMING POOLS

Porchester Baths   (101/D6)
Turkish-style Art Nouveau indoor swimming pool with wonderful tiles and fittings. It may have lost some of its splendour, but a visit is well worth it and still a wonderful experience – and there is lots of room. Sauna, steam baths. *Men only: Mon, Wed, Sat 9 am–10 pm; women only: Tues, Thurs, Fri 9 am–10 pm; accomp. by partner: Sun; Price: £13.95, extra charge for massage; Queensway; Tel: 0171-798 36 89; Underground: Queensway*

The Sanctuary   (104/A5)
Women only, ideal after a shopping trip. Luxurious basement health centre with a tropical flair. *Mon–Fri 10 am–10 pm, Sat 10 am–6 pm. Price: £39.50 for a whole day, after 5 pm £27.50; 11 Floral Street; Tel: 0171-240 96 35; Underground: Covent Garden*

THEATRES

London has also got lots to offer here – famous actors such as Dustin Hoffman come for a season because they enjoy treading the boards with 'Shakespearean actors'. Many British actors and actresses have become world-famous: Charlie Chaplin, Richard Burton, Laurence Olivier, Emma Thompson, Vanessa Redgrave. And where else in the world are actors awarded a title?

As well as the National Theatre in the South Bank Arts Centre, which actually consists of three different theatres, the Royal Shakespeare Company performs at the Barbican Centre during the winter and there are about 50 commercial theatres in the West End (*Shaftesbury Avenue, Haymarket, Strand*). In addition there are numerous fringe and pub theatres (experimental productions). The price of theatre tickets ranges from £7 to £30. The Half Price Ticket Booth in Leicester Square sells tickets for performances on the same day at half price. It is open from 12 noon. Many of the theatres have matinée performances, especially at weekends, which are usually not as fully booked. Note that drinks for the interval can often be ordered and paid for in advance – and are then waiting for you in a pre-arranged place.

The Donmar Warehouse (104/A5)
New plays and interesting audiences. Next to it is the *Detroit Bar*, a trendy meeting place. The best cocktails can be bought here and there is a mini-restaurant in the basement. *35 Earlham Street; Tel: 0171-867 11 50; Underground: Covent Garden*

Globe Theatre (113/E1)
Shakespeare's theatre recently reconstructed in original style. *Exhibition open May–Sept Tues–Sat 9 am–4 pm (closed 12.30 pm–2 pm), Mon 9 am–4 pm, Sun 9 am–2.30 pm. Daily performances. New Globe Walk, Bankside; Tel: 0171-928 64 06; Underground: Mansion House/London Bridge*

Haymarket (111/F1)
One of the most elegant theatre in London. Platinum bar, chic audiences. *Haymarket; Tel: 0171-930 98 32; Underground: Piccadilly Circus*

Open Air Theatre & Opera (102/C2)
Open-air Shakespeare productions in the summer. *Inner Circle, Regent's Park; Tel: 0171-935 58 84; Underground: Baker Street*

Palladium (103/E5)
Beautiful former Victorian music hall. *Argyll Street; Tel: 0171-437 73 73; Underground: Oxford Circus*

Royal Court (110/B5)
⭑ Well known for its innovative productions. Temporarily closed . *Sloane Square; Tel: 0171-730 17 45; Underground: Sloane Square*

Royal National Theatre (112/B1)
There are always interesting plays on here. *South Bank; Tel: 0171-928 22 52; Underground: Waterloo*

Royal Shakespeare Company (105/E4)
The Barbican Centre; Tel: 0171-638 88 91; Underground: Barbican

The Theatre Royal (104/B5)
★ Elegant decor, situated in the middle of Covent Garden. *Drury Lane; Underground: Covent Garden.*

London at close quarters

These walks are marked in green on the map outside back flap and in the street atlas beginning on page 100

① A ROMANTIC EVENING STROLL FROM THE CITY'S OUTSKIRTS TO PARLIAMENT

View historic as well as modern buildings on both sides of the Thames and take a break in the interesting pubs and restaurants on the way.

Start with a quick visit to the cosy *Black Friar* pub. It is quite unique in London with its Art Nouveau interior composed of lots of marble, mahogany and mosaics. It may be small but it is well worth a visit (**104/D6**). It is situated between Black Friars Lane and New Bridge Street in Black Friars Court (on the corner) (Underground: Blackfriars). From here go in the direction of Black Friars Bridge. Your next target, the *Oxo Tower* with a restaurant on the eighth floor (page 51), is on the opposite side of the river. Turn right along the bank of the Thames after crossing the bridge and follow the grey arrows on the wall, which will lead you to your destination. Do not be put off by the authoritative manner of the doorman who guards the entrance and the lift. There is a wonderful view of London from the eighth floor and also from a visitors' viewing platform. Don't forget to try the expensive but very good cocktails.

The lift takes you into a rather uninspiring forecourt. On your right is Barge House Street, which leads to Upper Ground, a street running parallel to the river. To get back to the Thames turn right again and continue to *Coin Street Cooperative Market* for which there are large signs but which is actually only a collection of alternative shops (although it includes an excellent pizzeria). From here you turn left along the bank of the Thames towards Waterloo Bridge (**112/B1**). You will come to the *South Bank complex* (page 78), which consists of the National Theatre and various concert halls. The futuristic building opposite is Charing Cross Station (**112/B2**). Follow the river round to Westminster Bridge (**112/B2**), where the majestic *County Hall*

(112/B2), the former administrative headquarters of the Council of Greater London, is situated.

It now houses an elegant Marriott Hotel – with a wonderful view of Big Ben – and the London Aquarium. With some luck and very good timing you can watch the sun set behind *Big Ben* and the *Houses of Parliament*. The Mother of Parliaments is seen at its best when floodlit at night. After surveying the scene with suitable admiration cross Westminster Bridge and then turn right along the Victoria Embankment, where *Cleopatra's Needle* (pages 16–17) stands (112/A2). Late in the evening when there is not so much traffic it is possible to sit here peacefully on one of the ornamental benches on the bank of the River Thames and enjoy the wonderful panorama of this metropolis.

② THE FINANCIAL DISTRICT

Experience a mixture of medieval lanes, beautiful churches and famous institutions, such as Lloyd's or the Bank of England.

The most powerful district in the whole of Great Britain is an area full of contrasts: the Stock Exchange, various financial markets, narrow medieval lanes and famous churches designed by Christopher Wren and Nicholas Hawksmoor and other well known architects.

Subject to its own regulations, London's financial centre has a very self-assured air – everyone here seems aware of his own value. We start off at Tower Hill Underground Station (114/B1) (Fenchurch Street exit) and ex-plore this area by way of side streets, which reveal its medieval character. On the left of Cooper's Row is Trinity Square, cross Trinity Square Gardens and then turn into Savage Gardens from where a left turn brings you into *Pepys Street.* This is where Samuel Pepys, the famous diarist who described the Fire of London, used to live. In the church of *St Olave* there is a list of the 25 wards in the Corporation of the City of London, which elects the Lord Mayor.

Turn into Seething Lane, which runs between Hart Street and Pepys Street, and carry on to Crutched Friars. At the far end turn left and then right and go up the stairs into New London Street. Go across the forecourt of Fenchurch Street Underground Station as well as Fenchurch Street itself and into Billiter Street, then turn left into Fenchurch Avenue. From here you have a view of the controversial new *Lloyd's Building* (page 18), which was designed by Richard Rogers, the architect of the Centre Pompidou in Paris. Turn left along Lime Street until you come to *Leadenhall Market.* This is worth a visit at lunch-time not only for its atmosphere of bustling activity but also for its architecture, since it is a wonderful Victorian, cast-iron structure. Continue via the Bull's Head Passage and Gracechurch Street to the Bell Inn Yard and then turn right into St Michael's Alley. There are two buildings here that should not be missed: *St Michael-upon-Cornhill,* a church designed by Christopher Wren in the simple style which is so typical of his work, and the *Jamaica*

Wine House (Tel: 0171-629 94 96), where the pleasure is more worldly, although it is often only open at lunchtime.

If you go left past St Michael's you will come to the Caterers' guild hall, which unfortunately can only be viewed from the outside. Then head for Castle Court, where the oldest pub in the city, *The George & Vulture* (page 84), is situated. Simple traditional fare is served here at lunch time.

Go in the direction of Cornhill (**106/A5**), which is the continuation of Leadenhall Street, via Castle Court and Birchin Lane. Cornhill brings you to the Bank Underground Station. Turn right here past the *Royal Exchange Building*.

In Lothbury take a look at *St Margaret's Lothbury,* one of Wren's churches with beautiful 17th-century woodwork. House No. 7, which is situated beside it, is a marvellous example of Victorian architecture.

Turn left again and continue straight ahead until you reach Threadneedle Street, where the Bank of England stands. Another left turn brings you into Victoria Street from where you can see *Mansion House*, the Lord Mayor's official residence. The interior, especially the Egyptian Hall, is worth seeing, but written permission must be obtained first.

Two more left turns and you come to Walbrook, where one of the most beautiful churches designed by Wren, *St Stephen Walbrook*, can be admired. It includes an altar by Henry Moore. Return to Queen Victoria Street and bear across Garlick Hill and Bow Church Yard to the church of *St Mary-le-Bow* (page 23). It used to be said that all 'true' Cockneys were born within the sound of Bow bells. For those who are now hungry: *Sweetings*, London's oldest fish restaurant is an obvious choice (page 50). For those who still have enough energy: follow on with a tour of *St Paul's Cathedral* (page 25). It is only ten minutes away and well worth seeing.

③ A SUNDAY STROLL FOR ANY DAY OF THE WEEK

Here there is a mixture of nature and science, park and museum. You can decide what you would prefer to do: visit one of London's loveliest parks, go to Madame Tussaud's or follow the trail of Sherlock Holmes.

Since many places of interest in London are closed on Sunday mornings, it is a good idea to visit *Hyde Park* (page 31) first. Depending on how much energy you have, you can either start off at the Serpentine Lake (**110/A2**) (Underground: Hyde Park Corner) and walk through the park to *Speaker's Corner* or get off the Underground at Marble Arch. Be warned: distances which may seem short on the map can take at least half an hour to walk.

The first 'speakers' start to arrive at about eleven o'clock. Expect to hear orators who can become excited about everything under the sun. Most hold very strong beliefs about their given topic. Listeners are free to heartily vocalize their opinions. Perhaps, it isn't the truest form of debating, but it all still provides good entertainment.

Carry on into the *Edgware Road* (**102/B5**) – there is a small Lebanese community here and lots to admire and try in the shops, e.g. fresh mango juice, crunchy honey-cakes, almond pastries and salads in Manoush's Juice Bar. Afterwards, either continue along the Edgware Road as far as *Marylebone Road* – or thread your way through side streets lined with elegant and ornately decorated houses such as those in Bickenhall Street until you reach Marylebone Road. Here you pass *Madame Tussaud's* (page 42) which is a very popular tourist attraction. Further along the way you come to *Queen Mary's Gardens*, where there are hundreds of roses and other beautiful flowers in a garden laid out opposite Regent's College. The best way to get there is to go past Madame Tussaud's in the direction of York Gate, then turn left at the traffic lights, cross over a little bridge, the York Bridge, which will bring you to *Regent's Park* (page 32). Regent's College (**102/C2**) is on your left. Go through the wrought-iron gates towards the fountain. On the left is the Open Air Theatre, where performances are held in the summer (May–Sept), and on the right is a typically English country garden, where the flowers look as if they are growing wild but they have actually all been very carefully placed.

From here you can continue to the *Zoo* or turn sharp right and you will find yourself at the centre of Queen Mary's Gardens – which is a mass of blossom from the middle to the end of June. It is tempting to have a rest and spend a little time here beside the little lake. For the legwary, a deck-chair costs 70 p for four hours.

Those who have not yet had enough of gardens are advised to cross the road beside the cafeteria and to take a seat in the *Holme Green* part of the park, where there are often concerts on Sundays (see notice-board). This is where the IRA carried out their attack on the military band. Leave the park by Clarence Gate and admire the *Regency terraces* designed by *John Nash*, who intended re-creating his country lifestyle in the capital. Fortunatly he was only permitted to build eight of the 56 villas he had planned – otherwise not very much of the park would have been left. In the background is the copper roof of the London Mosque. Turn left into Baker Street before reaching Clarence Terrace and you will now have entered *Sherlock Holmes country*. 'His' house at 221 b Baker Street was turned into the *Sherlock Holmes Museum* in 1990 *(Tel: 0171-935 8866)*, which you are sure to find a memorable experience. If that's not enough you can meet up with a 'descendant of the famous detective'. Just give him a ring: *Steward Quentin Holmes, Tel: 0171-724 72 15*. For a fee *(£ 1 per person)* he allows himself to be photographed in full costume. On Tuesdays and Thursdays he is always to be found at the Baker Street Underground Station. You can purchase a book of mysteries and tales of the famous detective in the shop called *Sherlock Holmes Memorabilia & Co*. This makes a good little present to take back home with you.

Practical information

Useful addresses and indispensable tips for your visit to London

CUSTOMS

The following goods may be imported without incurring customs duty: travellers arriving from EU countries with duty paid goods: 800 cigarettes, 1 kg tobacco, 90 litres of wine, 110 litres of beer and 10 litres of spirits. Travellers from non-EU countries or with goods bought duty free within the EU: 200 cigarettes or 250g of tobacco, 1 litre of alcoholic beverages stronger than 22% proof or 2 litres of fortified or sparkling wine or other liqueurs, 2 litres of still table wine. Heavy penalties are imposed for any attempt to import animals, plants or drugs.

DOCTORS AND PHARMACIES

Emergency Tel: 999 (free of charge) for police, fire or ambulance. Every hospital has a casualty department where emergency cases are treated free of charge. An appointment is not necessary, but you may have to wait a long time. You can call a private doctor at *Doctor call Tel: 0181-900 10 00*. Doctor's fee and prescriptions from £ 60. Your hotel can give you the name of a private doctor.

Bliss Chemist   (102/B5)
Pharmacy with long opening hours. *5 Marble Arch; Tel: 0171-723 61 16; Underground: Marble Arch*

Natureworks   (102/C5)
Health centre for holistic medicine. *16 Balderton Street; Tel: 0171-355 40 36; Underground: Bond Street*

Underwood   (109/D1)
Another pharmacy chain with long opening hours. *114 Queensway; Tel: 0171-229 11 83; Underground: Queensway*

DRIVING IN LONDON

Tourists from abroad should always take care to drive on the left. At roundabouts traffic coming from the right has priority. Sound your horn only in a real emergency. Multi-storey and underground car parks are very expensive, about £ 20 for 24 hours. It is cheaper further out of the centre. If your car has been fixed by a 'clamp', phone *0171-*

252 22 22 for instructions. AA Automobile Club: *Tel: 0800-88 77 66* (free of charge).

EMBASSIES

Canadian High Commission(102/C6)
1 Grosvenor Square; Tel: 0171-258 66 00; Fax: 258 65 33; Underground: Marble Arch/Bond Street

Embassy of the
United States of America (102/C6)
24 Grosvenor Square; Tel: 0171-499 90 00; web site: http://www.usembassy.org.uk; Underground: Marble Arch/Bond Street

EVENTS

The magazines *Time Out* and *What's On* are published weekly. The *Evening Standard* and the Sunday papers also list events and include an entertainment guide.

HAIRDRESSERS

Antenna (108/C2)
For the brave: very trendy! *27A Kensington Church Street; Tel: 0171-938 18 66; Underground: High Street Kensington*

Bambu (103/E5)
Reasonable prices, but simple styles. *17 Foubert's Place/corner of Carnaby Street; Tel: 0171-734 44 65*

John Frieda (112/D1)
Celebrities' hairdressers. *Ritz Hotel, Piccadilly; Tel: 0171-493 45 75; Underground: Green Park*

Trevor Sorbie (104/B5)
Fashionable styles, friendly. *10 Russell Street; Tel: 0171-379 69 01; Underground: Covent Garden*

Geo F. Trumper (110/C1)
Traditional barber. *9 Curzon Street; Tel: 0171-499 29 32; Underground: Green Park*

INFORMATION

British Tourist Authority
(Web site: http//www.visitbritain.com)

In Canada:
Suite 450, 111 Avenue Road, Toronto, Ontario M5R 3J8; Tel: 416- 925 6326; Fax: 416- 961 2175

In USA:
7th Floor, 551 Fifth Avenue, New York, NY 10176-0799; Tel: 212-986 2266; Fax: 212- 986 1188

INFORMATION IN LONDON

British Visitor Centre (103/E6)
Mon–Fri 9 am–6.30 pm, Sat–Sun 10 am –6 pm; 1 Regent Street; Tel: 0171-839 24 70; Underground: Piccadilly Circus

London Tourist Board
Information Centre
Victoria Station (111/D4)
Station forecourt. Accommodation booking service (small fee charged). Information leaflets, free Underground and bus timetables. Travel bookshop. *Daily 8 am–7 pm, reduced opening times Nov–Easter; Tel: 0171-824 88 44. For accommodation booking (credit cards only) Tel: 0171-932 20 20*
Other Tourist Information Centres:

Harrods (110/B3)
Information about bus tours organized by Harrods (base-

ment). *Mon, Tues, Thurs, and Fri 9 am–5.30 pm, Wed, Sat 9 am–7 pm; Brompton Road; Underground: Knightsbridge*

Selfridges (102 /C5)
Mon, Tues, Wed, Fri, Sat 9 am– 5.30 pm, Thurs 9.30 am–7 pm; Oxford Street; Underground: Marble Arch/Bond Street

Heathrow Airport (O)
All the information about train and bus travel in Great Britain is available here, as well as general accommodation and theatre ticket booking services. *Daily 9 am–6 pm*

LOST PROPERTY

All lost property should be reported to the police so that insurance claims can be validated. Every British Rail station has a 'Lost Property' Office.

London Transport
Lost Property Office (102/B4)
200 Baker Street; Mon–Fri 9.30 am–2 pm; Tel: 0171-833 09 96. If you leave your belongings in a taxi: *15 Penton Street; Underground: Angel*

MONEY

It is cheaper to change money at a bank; hotels and exchange offices often charge high commission rates. An address in London is usually required in order to change money and sometimes you may be asked to show your passport. Banks are open Mon–Fri from 9.30 am to 3.30 pm. Some branches of the major banks are also open on Sat 9.30 am to 12 pm.

PASSPORTS & VISAS

A valid passport is sufficient for citizens of Australia, Canada and the USA. Visitors from EU countries are required to have an identity document. Passports should be valid for at least six months beyond the period of the intended stay.

POST & TELEPHONES

It is possible to phone almost anywhere direct from a public telephone and even to be rung back there by the person you have called. From London the country code for the USA and Canada is 001. From abroad the country code for Great Britain is 0044. Directory enquiries for London is 142, for the rest of Great Britain 192. International directory enquiries 153. If you have further difficulties or quiries call the operator: 100.

Since 1995 the area code for London has been either 0171 or 0181; you have to dial this even when phoning from within London. When phoning from abroad remember to dial 0044 first and then the London area code.

As well as coin operated telephones there are also telephones that can only be operated using a phone card. Phone cards cost from £1 to £10 and can be purchased at post offices and newsagents. Post office opening hours: *Mon–Fri 9 am–5.30 pm, Sat 9 am– 12.30 pm*

Main Post Office (112/A1)
Trafalgar Square, St Martin's Place; Mon–Sat 8 am–8 pm, Sun 10 am–5 pm, also keeps letters to be called for; Underground: Charing Cross

Boats

You can take a boat trip on the River Thames from Westminster Pier *(Tel: 0171-930 40 97)*, Tower Pier *(Tel: 0171-488 03 44)* and Charing Cross Pier *(Tel: 0171-839 33 12)*. Cruises on the Regent's Canal are also available from: *Canal Cruises, Tel: 0171-482 25 50; Zoo Waterbus, Tel: 0171-485 44 33; Jason's Canal Cruises, Tel: 0171-286 34 28.* All cruises leave from *Camden Lock; Underground: Camden Town*

Underground and Buses

The quickest way to get around London is the Underground, the *tube.* Journeys by bus offer the added bonus of sightseeing, but it takes much longer to reach your destination. Underground maps are available at every Underground station, bus timetables at tourist information centres and Underground stations. 24-hour telephone information service: *Tel: 0171-222 12 34.* Red double-decker buses run throughout central London and its suburbs, although they are currently being replaced by

Still a familiar sight throughout London — an old-fashioned telephone box

94

smaller buses. There are express Red Arrow buses between Westminster and Victoria (route C 1) from Mondays to Saturdays, which operate on a flat-fare system.

The *Docklands Light Railway* runs from Tower Gateway to Island Gardens in the Docklands on an elevated track. Alternatively you can take bus D 1 or D 2 from Waterloo, but they only run from 9 am to 6.30 pm. Please check that your ticket is valid for this zone.

The Underground becomes extremely crowded in rush hours (8 am–9 am and 5 pm–7 pm). Escalators are often not in operation and the long, steep stairs are difficult to climb for those who cannot walk very well.There is only one class in the Underground. Smoking is not allowed. Watch out for pickpockets, especially when it is very busy. Trains run frequently between 5.30 am and midnight (7.30 am to 11.30 pm on Sundays).

There are twelve different lines, each identified by a different colour and the name of the terminus. It is therefore relatively easy to find your way around on the Underground. Single tickets cost between £ 1.10 and £ 2.20, depending on the distance covered. Substantial savings can be made by purchasing a One Day Travelcard (£ 3.50, can only be used after 9.30 am) or a One Day London Travel (LT) Card (can be used before 9.30 am). A passport photograph is required for a Weekly Travelcard (£ 15). Travelcards are valid on all lines in central London (£ 3).

SIGHTSEEING TOURS AND GUIDED WALKS

Organized tours in red double-decker buses take you past all London's principle sights. In summer, these buses have an open upper deck, weather permitting. They run daily every half hour between 10 am and 5 pm from Piccadilly Circus. A ticket costs £ 10, or £ 8 if you buy it at a London Tourist Board Information Centre. Harrods also organizes sightseeing tours with comfortable little buses. They depart daily at 10 am, 1 pm and 4 pm, £ 17. For those who would rather plan a bus trip for themselves, contact London Transport Information *Tel: 0171-222 12 34.*

Several companies offer conducted walking tours, e. g. *Historical Walks, Tel: 0181-668 40 19.* Information on the back page of the *Times,* in *Time Out* and *What's On.* Original London Walks offers a different walk every day from April until December. Starting point is usually one of the Underground stations. *(Tel: 0171-624 39 78).* These tours provide profound insights but they are time-consuming. An adventurous but pleasant way of getting to know London and some of the local people is with Ghost Tours, for about £ 10, Tel: 0171-256 89 37; time and place vary.

STREET ATLAS

London A–Z
The best street index of London. It is available in paperback from all kiosks, newsagents and bookshops.

TAXIS

The public transport system in London is on a par with any large European city of this size even though it might not seem that way at first.

Just as famous as the double-decker buses, the taxis can be hailed anywhere in the street when the yellow *for hire* sign is illuminated. There are taxi queues in front of hotels and stations. A meter inside the vehicle registers the fare.

An extra charge is made for a fourth passenger, luggage and late-night journeys. The driver expects a 15% tip, on which he has to pay tax. For women who would rather be driven by a woman there is a taxi company called *Ladybirds, Tel: 0181-390 82 82 and 399 74 74.*

TIPPING

As a general rule 15% of the bill should be given as a tip; cloakroom and washroom attendants should not be given less than 10 p. Hairdressers £2–£5. Hall porters or commissionaires can be very helpful when it comes to buying tickets or gaining entry to clubs and they expect a tip of at least £1.

TIME ZONES

Great Britain runs on Greenwich Mean Time (GMT), which is one hour behind Central European Time.

VOLTAGE

Voltage 230 V.; remember to bring an adapter.

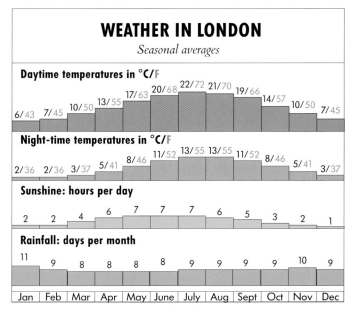

WEATHER IN LONDON
Seasonal averages

Daytime temperatures in °C/F

Jan	Feb	Mar	Apr	May	June	July	Aug	Sept	Oct	Nov	Dec
6/43	7/45	10/50	13/55	17/63	20/68	22/72	21/70	19/66	14/57	10/50	7/45

Night-time temperatures in °C/F

Jan	Feb	Mar	Apr	May	June	July	Aug	Sept	Oct	Nov	Dec
2/36	2/36	3/37	5/41	8/46	11/52	13/55	13/55	11/52	8/46	5/41	3/37

Sunshine: hours per day

Jan	Feb	Mar	Apr	May	June	July	Aug	Sept	Oct	Nov	Dec
2	2	4	6	7	7	7	6	5	3	2	1

Rainfall: days per month

Jan	Feb	Mar	Apr	May	June	July	Aug	Sept	Oct	Nov	Dec
11	9	8	8	8	8	9	9	9	9	10	9

Do's and don'ts

*Useful tips and advise on how to avoid
some of the traps and pitfalls that
await the unwary traveller*

Going out

It is very difficult to find a good restaurant in London that is open on a Sunday. Try 'ethnic cuisine' in Soho instead. Theatre and opera tickets should be bought as far in advance as possible. Some returns are available, but there are rarely enough for everybody waiting at the box office. And touts (or scalpers) are a plague! They sell cheap, sometimes even forged, tickets at greatly inflated prices. Try phoning the theatre or asking the hall porter in your hotel, even if he does charge commission just like the agencies.

Drinks

Some hotels in the higher price category only sell double whiskies, gins etc, which not only go to your head very quickly but also rapidly drains your purse!

Politeness

Englishmen like to be regarded as gentlemen and treated accordinly. Therefore, when in England , do as the English. Foreign visitors should always remember that it helps to apologize often in Britain and to wrap up questions in polite phrases. Some Britons even apologize when *you* stand on *their* feet! The general volume tends to be muted – after all, no one wants to be regarded as a hooligan ...

Dress

It may be hard to imagine, but in the London of punkers and 'house' music a jacket and tie are required for afternoon tea in the better hotels. This is still one of the traditional rituals of the Brittish and will be for a long time to come. Customers in jeans and running shoes are not welcome.

Parking

Driving in London is difficult enough for residents who are in possession of a parking permit. For tourists, on the other hand, parking is a nightmare – either horribly expensive or absolutely impossible. Illegally parked cars are towed away very quickly, even a bus can disappear in a few minutes, and it costs a lot of time and money to recover them. So this is to be avoided if at all pos-

Taxis in Leicester Square

sible. London traffic police's latest hobby is clamping. Clamps are fixed to a wheel of the car so that it is no longer manoeuvrable. A £ 48 fine (as well as the cost of the paperwork involved) has to be paid at a police station. After the wheels of justice have taken their coarse, which can take hours, a company appears to remove the clamps.

Piccadilly Circus
During the day just a congested traffic junction, which can quite easely be avoided although the Trocadero has lots to offer if the weather is bad, or it rains. But at night, lit up by huge neon signs, it becomes the exciting Piccadilly that everyone imagines.

Restaurants
The addition of a cover charge to the bill is a popular means of making the menu appear cheaper at first – the shock then comes with the bill. A 15% service charge is also often not included in the price. Check this as well as your credit card counterfoil, where the total is left open inviting you to pay another tip.

Soho
Take care when frequenting the Soho area – what is on offer there is often not worth the money. So-called 'private clubs' ask for a membership fee (about £ 10) at the door, drinks are almost just as expensive. The performances of the 'dancers' or 'entertainers' are rarely worth this investment. The best club, Raymonds Revue Bar in Walkers Court, is tame, expensive and touristy.

Taxis
Use only the black cabs in central London, i.e. the old-fashioned vehicles with a high roof. Drivers of other types of car also offer their services, but they are only licensed as 'radio taxis'. They are only allowed to collect passengers who have phoned to order them. It is best to avoid any offers made by drivers of these mini cabs at airports and stations, since they are usually over expensive. Mini cabs are also often underinsured. Real London cabbies are reliable, know London inside-out and expect a 15% tip.

Last, but not least
The golden rule for foreign visitors is: always stand in line! The British queue everywhere – not only at bus stops, but also in front of theatres and cinemas and even in shops. Pushing to the front of the queue is not only impolite here, it will gain you some very black looks. Life in London is not as hectic as in some other big cities, but it is still important to muster the necessary patience!

Street Atlas of London

*Please refer to back cover for an overview
of this street atlas*

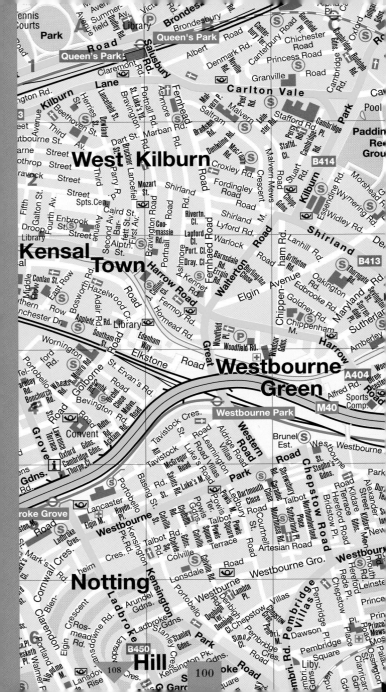

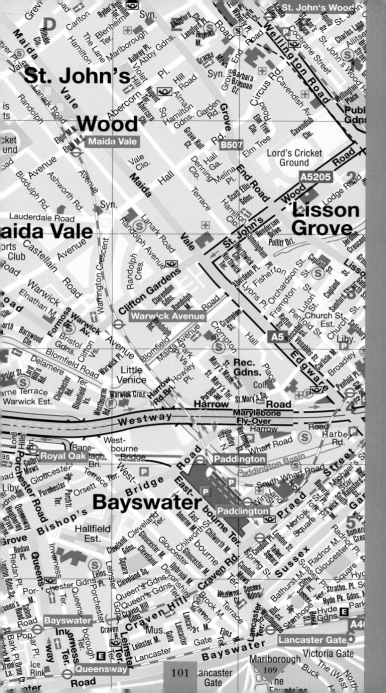

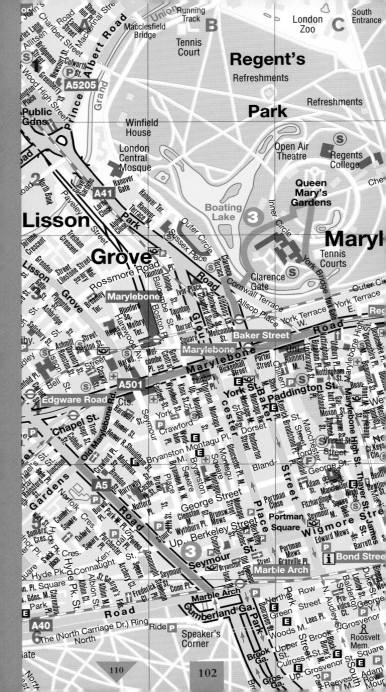

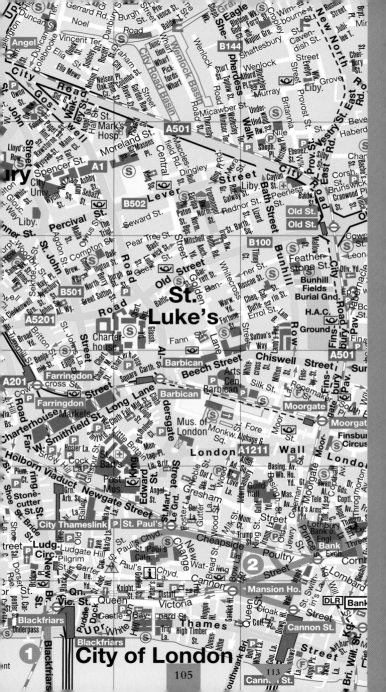

City of London

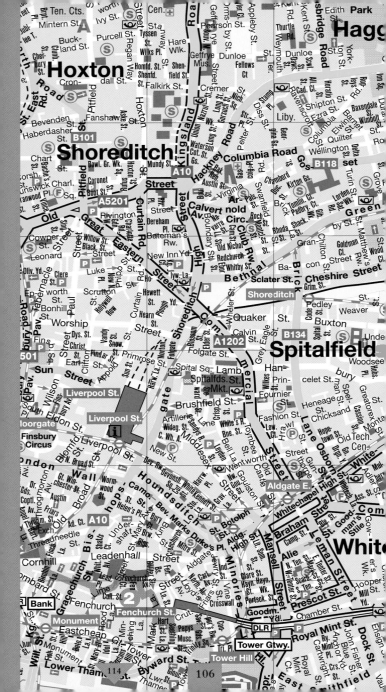

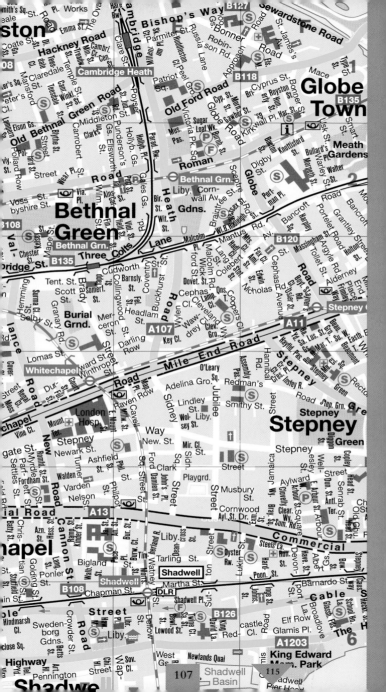

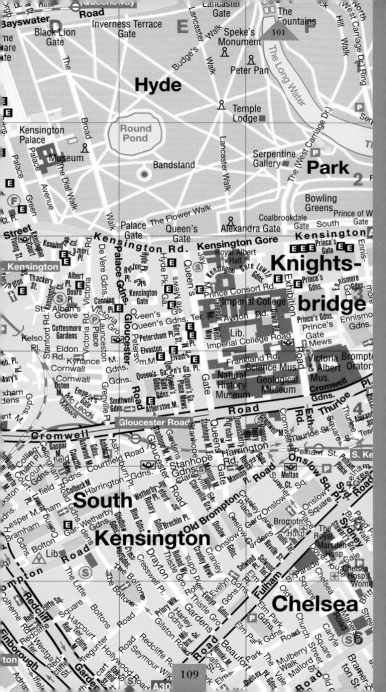

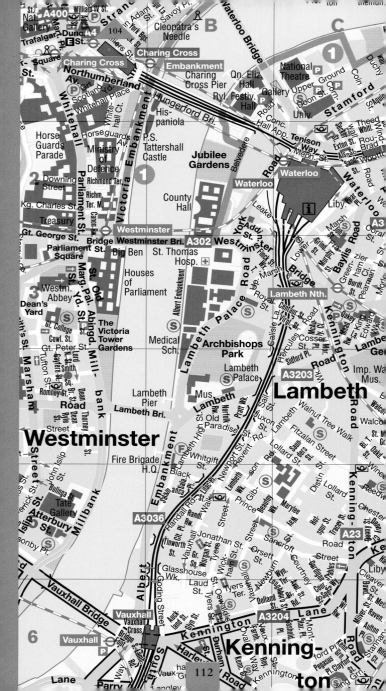

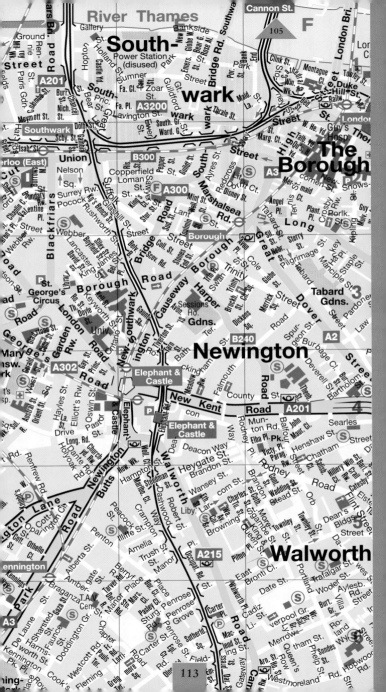

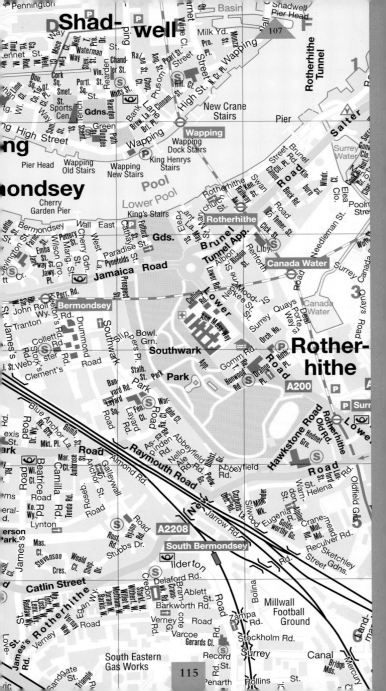

STREET ATLAS LEGEND

Autobahn mit Nummer Motorway with number		**i**	Tourist-Information Tourist information centre
Schnellstraße/Bundesstraße Motor highway/Federal road		⊞	ⓈⒺ Krankenhaus/Schule Hospital/School
Hauptstraße Mainroad		Ⓕ Ⓟ	Feuerwehr/Polizei Fire station/Police station
Übrige Straßen/Weg Other roads/Footpath		⚊ ⚠	Campingplatz/Jugendherberge Camping site/Youth hostel
Straßen in Bau/Planung Roads under construction/projected		⌦	Post Post office
Fußgängerzone/Einbahnstraße Pedestrian zone/One-way street		♀	Försterei Forester's lodge
Eisenbahn mit Bahnhof Railway with station		♀ ♣	Einzelne Bäume Isolated trees
Güter- und Industriebahn Freight and industrial railway		⚲ ⚡	Sendeanlage/Leuchtturm Transmitting station/Lighthouse
U7 U6 U-Bahn/Stadtbahn Ⓜ Underground/Light Rail		♙ ☆ ✗	Denkmal/Mühle/Windmühle Monument/Mill/Windmill
641 Bus/Straßenbahn mit Endhaltestelle 698 Bus/Tramway with terminus		🄺 🄱 🄲 🄴 🄲 🄰	Konsulat/Botschaft Consulate/Embassy
Fähre Ferry		🅿 🅿 🅿	Parkplatz/Parkhaus/Tiefgarage Car park/Parking house/Under-ground car park
Wald/Park Forest/Park		🏊	Hallenbad Indoor swimming pool
Friedhof, Weinberg Cemetery, Vineyard			500 m ———————— 1000 ft

---

Marco Polo Walking Routes

❶ A Romantic Evening Stroll from the City's Outskirts to Parliament

❷ The Financial District

❸ A Sunday Stroll for any Day of the Week

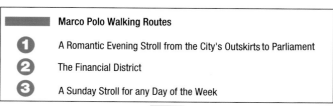

This index lists a selection of the streets and squares shown in the street atlas